ARCHITECTURAL DESIGN

EDITORIAL OFFICES:
42 LEINSTER GARDENS, LONDON W2 3AN
TEL: 071-402 2141 FAX: 071-723 9540

EDITOR: Maggie Toy
EDITORIAL TEAM: Iona Spens, Pip Vice, Katherine MacInnes
ART EDITOR: Andrea Bettella
CHIEF DESIGNER: Mario Bettella
DESIGNER: Jan Richter

CONSULTANTS: Catherine Cooke, Terry Farrell, Kenneth Frampton, Charles Jencks, Heinrich Klotz, Leon Krier, Robert Maxwell, Demetri Porphyrios, Kenneth Powell, Colin Rowe, Derek Walker

SUBSCRIPTION OFFICES:
UK: VCH PUBLISHERS (UK) LTD
8 WELLINGTON COURT, WELLINGTON STREET
CAMBRIDGE CB1 1HZ
TEL: (0223) 321111 FAX: (0223) 313321

USA AND CANADA: VCH PUBLISHERS INC
303 NW 12TH AVENUE DEERFIELD BEACH,
FLORIDA 33442-1788 USA
TEL: (305) 428-5566 / (800) 367-8249
FAX: (305) 428-8201

ALL OTHER COUNTRIES:
VCH VERLAGSGESELLSCHAFT MBH
BOSCHSTRASSE 12, POSTFACH 101161
69451 WEINHEIM
FEDERAL REPUBLIC OF GERMANY
TEL: 06201 606 148 FAX: 06201 606 184

© 1994 Academy Group Ltd. All rights reserved. No part of this publication may be reproduced or transmitted in any form or by any means, electronic or mechanical, including photocopying, recording or any information storage or retrieval system without permission in writing from the Publishers. Neither the Editor nor the Academy Group hold themselves responsible for the opinions expressed by writers of articles or letters in this magazine. The Editor will give careful consideration to unsolicited articles, photographs and drawings; please enclose a stamped addressed envelope for their return (if required). Payment for material appearing in AD is not normally made except by prior arrangement. All reasonable care will be taken of material in the possession of AD and agents and printers, but they regret that they cannot be held responsible for any loss or damage.
Architectural Design is published six times per year (Jan/Feb; Mar/Apr; May/Jun; Jul/Aug; Sept/Oct; and Nov/Dec). Subscription rates for 1994 (incl p&p): Annual subscription price: UK only £65.00, World DM 195, USA $135.00 for regular subscribers. Student rate: UK only £50.00, World DM 156, USA$105.00 incl postage and handling charges. Individual issues: £14.95/DM 39.50 (plus £2.30/DM 5 for p&p, per issue ordered), US $24.95 (incl p&p).
Application to mail at second-class postage rates is pending at Deerfield Beach, FL. Postmaster. Send address changes to Architectural Design, 303 NW 12th Avenue, Deerfield Beach, FL 33442-1788. Printed in Italy. Origination by Print-Tek London. All prices are subject to change without notice. [ISSN: 0003-8504]

CONTENTS

ARCHITECTURAL DESIGN **MAGAZINE**
Battle & McCarthy Genesis of Natural Forces • *Ove Arup Partnership* Green Architecture • *Neil Spiller* When is a door not a door? • *Exhibitions* • *Books*

Spiller & Farmer research projects, 1993

ARCHITECTURAL DESIGN **PROFILE** No 110

ASPECTS OF MINIMAL ARCHITECTURE
Tadao **Ando** • Alberto **Campo Baeza** More with Less • Ricardo **Legorreta** • Claudio **Silvestrin** Architecture of Lessness • Jean **Nouvel** • Terry **Pawson** / Keith **Williams** Contextual Minimalism • Richard **Meier** • **Herzog** & **de Meuron** • Clare **Melhuish** On Minimalism in Architecture • Richard **Gluckman** • **Barto + Barto** • **Van Berkel** & **Bos** • Tony **Fretton** • Tod **Williams** & Billie **Tsien** • Pierre **d'Avoine** • Donald **Judd** • John **Pawson** • **Ushida** & **Findlay** • Katsuhiro **Isobe** • **O'Herlihy** + **Warner**

Ove Arup Partnership, New Parliamentary Buildings

Ricardo Legorreta, Hotel Camino Real, Mexico

BATTLE & McCARTHY
GENESIS OF NATURAL FORCES
MULTI-SOURCE SYNTHESIS

Higher technology architectural visions may go beyond the innovative application of known materials and technologies from other industries associated with the hardware of the industrial past. They should pursue the scientific revolution in the field of computer simulation of physical and environmental forces.

Technology transfer associated with our construction industry is, for example, less about taking the form and materials of an aeroplane, pulling off its wing and renaming it a house. It is more to do with using the air flow computer simulation programmes generated by the aircraft industry to predict the enhancement of natural ventilation with the aid of high level openings known as 'wind towers'. The efforts of such analysis may result in a form and use of materials which do not look 'high-tech' as we have come to know it, perhaps seem less clever, but certainly will be understood and appreciated as a more intelligent one.

The most decisive factors in 'form finding' a structure are involved with the interaction of materials with natural forces of gravity, wind, solar, light, sound, temperature and air movement: a materialisation of stresses following; strain yielding; deflection occurring; light being reflected and diffused; solar radiation being absorbed and re-radiated; air molecules moving from high to low pressure sources; sound being deflected and then absorbed, and so on.

Architecture has always been fired by the challenging comprehension of the interaction of materials with natural forces, whether it is dealing with a single natural force or many within a single form: *gravity* – from the construction of Stonehenge to the cantilever pylon of Calatrava's bridge for Seville; *wind* – from the aerodynamic shaping of Viking ships to Alsop's response to the mistral winds experienced by the Hotel du Departement for Marseilles; *solar* – from the Palm House of Kew to the latest solar collector glazing presently being developed by BP; *light* – from the dynamic light control devices for the central hall of La Villette to the science fiction satellite daylight reflectors which will orbit the globe providing endless daylight to all major centres of population; *temperature* – from the evaporative cooling techniques optimised by Alhambra's water features to the heat store techniques optimised by the Hong Kong Bank's major subterranean water tunnel to the sea; *air movement* – from the muskrats tunnelling technique which enhance natural ventilation due the air pressure differences induced by the low entrance and the high exit to the enormous cooling towers which grow from our landscape; *sound* – from Aalto's sound boxes to the dynamic structural form and acoustic space of the Manchester Concert Hall. Whatever our excuse, the domination of natural forces remains part of the human record.

Evolution of our understanding of natural forces interaction with materials: Given a set of natural forces, how may we form find with the sensitivity towards the quality inherent in structural materials which will eventually create an enclosure to the environmental comfort and satisfaction of the occupier with the minimum dependence upon valuable energy sources.

Like designers before him, Antonio Gaudi used hanging chain modelling techniques as a means of generating the primary structural form of the Guell Chapel in Barcelona. Experimenting with a series of upside-down wire models, in which the wires stood for columns and the attached bags of lead shot stood for the self-weight of the roof, Gaudi was able to form find an appropriate gravitational form. The unrestrained mechanism was free to move as the applied loads were varied until the final form within envelope of applied load fulfilled the design requirement. The form was then mapped out, inverted and finally built in stone.

This 'gravitational' sculptor's apparatus for generative form from physical forces can now be more accurately and rapidly achieved by computer form finding analysis such as the Fablon programme developed by Alistair Day and Terence Haslett of Arup. The finite element analysis computer programmes developed by the design studios of the manufacturing industry for measuring and understanding stress and strain flow intensity through structural components for all types of load cases, have now become a fundamental tool for structural analysis from the analysis of steel castings to concrete flat slabs of Owen William's Boots Factory and to Nervi largespan shell structures. In addition to the development of computational means of 'sculpting' physical forces, engineers have also provided architects with means of simulating the forces of light, sound, temperature and air movement with the use of advanced computer software handed

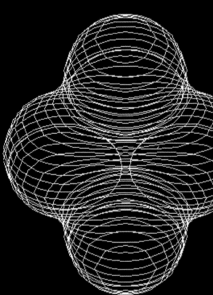

Initialised form

down by the aerospace industries.

This article aims to illustrate and demonstrate the potential use of computer simulation of natural forces on form based upon a hypothetical enclosure. The conception of the volume has been defined by a group of four 70m-diameter spheres contained within a single membrane. It has also been assumed that the structure is buoyant and is floating at sea on the equator. Admittedly the complexity of the brief for designing a building requires many forces other than natural forces such as function, social, economic and psychological forces. However, like Gaudi's gravitational experiments before us, the objective of this abstract demonstration is not to design a building but to create prototypes which demonstrate the architectural potential of using the latest computer software appliances for the simulation of natural forces which are waiting to be exploited for whatever the building type and its global location. The objective of the exercise is to form find a common structural enclosure where each of the natural forces may be co-ordinated without compromising its individual qualities. To solve this mystery, we first need to simulate, in as abstract a manner as possible, the force intensity of each of the primary natural forces and then try and reshape the structure in response to moderating these individual abstract forces. This process revealed three structural forms in harmony with the three primary forces of gravity, air molecular behaviour and radiation then by fusion single form was generated.

Sixteen forms are sought by the individual forces. To simplify the assessment, these were grouped under three types of forces: mechanical forces; radiation forces; air molecule forces. From these merged force diagrams, three new forms were established by co-ordinating the differences without eliminating the individual quality of each force. The only geometrical restraint was that the plan shape at the water level had to remain unchanged. The mechanical forces seek a pyramidal shape with a single peak and catinary sides. To minimise radiation gain the plan area should be minimised leading to straightening up of the sides with the flat roof. However, to ensure that good air movement is maintained, a number of high points are required. These new forms were then fused together by superimposing the computational forms by engineering judgement. The optimum form was thus generated. However, with more time and resources this composition of materials and form could have been extended to include more forces, and have been reviewed and assessed by computational 'random experience', whereby a variety of material passive and active properties could have been introduced into the analysis.

'One's vision is only as good as one's ability to justify that vision.' This design process was founded upon the intuitive form finding skill and knowledge of the design team's interpretation of the computer simulations. This analytical form finding approach, of investigating the theoretical form sought by each natural force, created a family of identifiable abstract forms into a network of compositions. These compositions were then merged by a sequence geometrical alignment towards an ideal composition.

Together with the inevitable conflicts between the demands of each force, an understanding of each natural force, performance geometry and materials, became the inspiration for architectural forms in terms of space, density and radiation. This approach may be the 'high-tech' architecture of the 90s. Computational simulation of natural forces is available and affordable. Architects may use such tools to expand their interpretation of natural forces with form. The engineering vocabulary of the architectural form of these abstract computer simulations does not claim to pose architectural solutions for the built form but claims to be a more realistic representation for predicting the future physical and environmental performance of the architecture than any artist's impression submitted in a planning submission.

The authors wish to thank Barnaby Gunning for his contribution to this article.

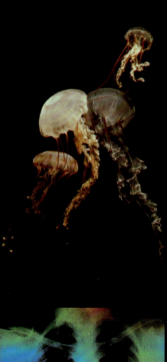

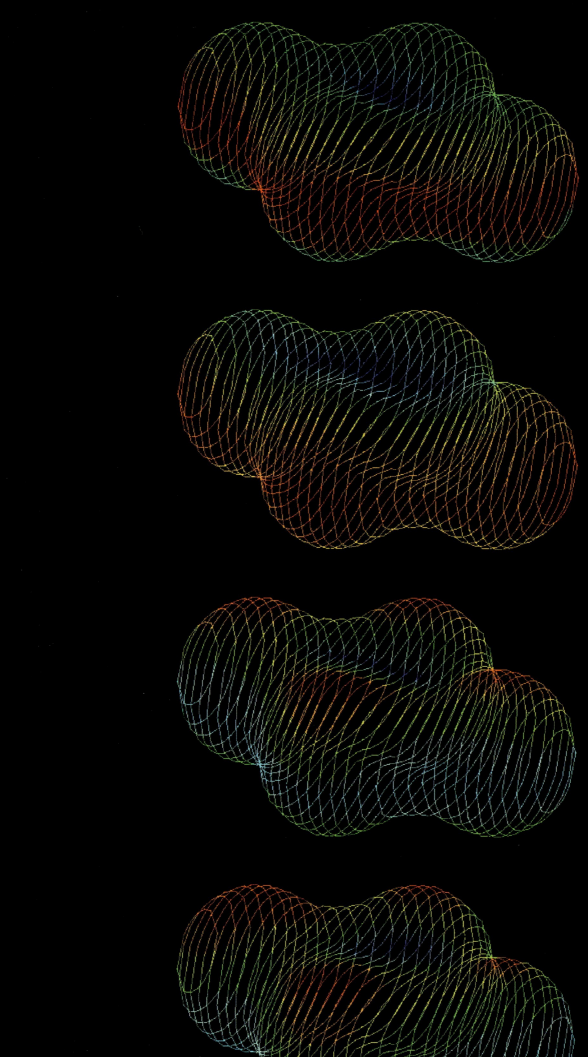
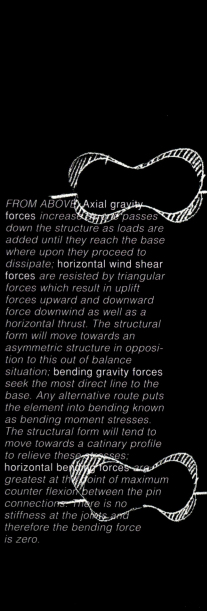

FROM ABOVE: Axial gravity forces increase as it passes down the structure as loads are added until they reach the base where upon they proceed to dissipate; **horizontal wind shear forces** are resisted by triangular forces which result in uplift forces upward and downward force downwind as well as a horizontal thrust. The structural form will move towards an asymmetric structure in opposition to this out of balance situation; **bending gravity forces** seek the most direct line to the base. Any alternative route puts the element into bending known as bending moment stresses. The structural form will tend to move towards a catinary profile to relieve these stresses; **horizontal bending forces are** greatest at the point of maximum counter flexion between the pin connections. There is no stiffness at the joints and therefore the bending force is zero.

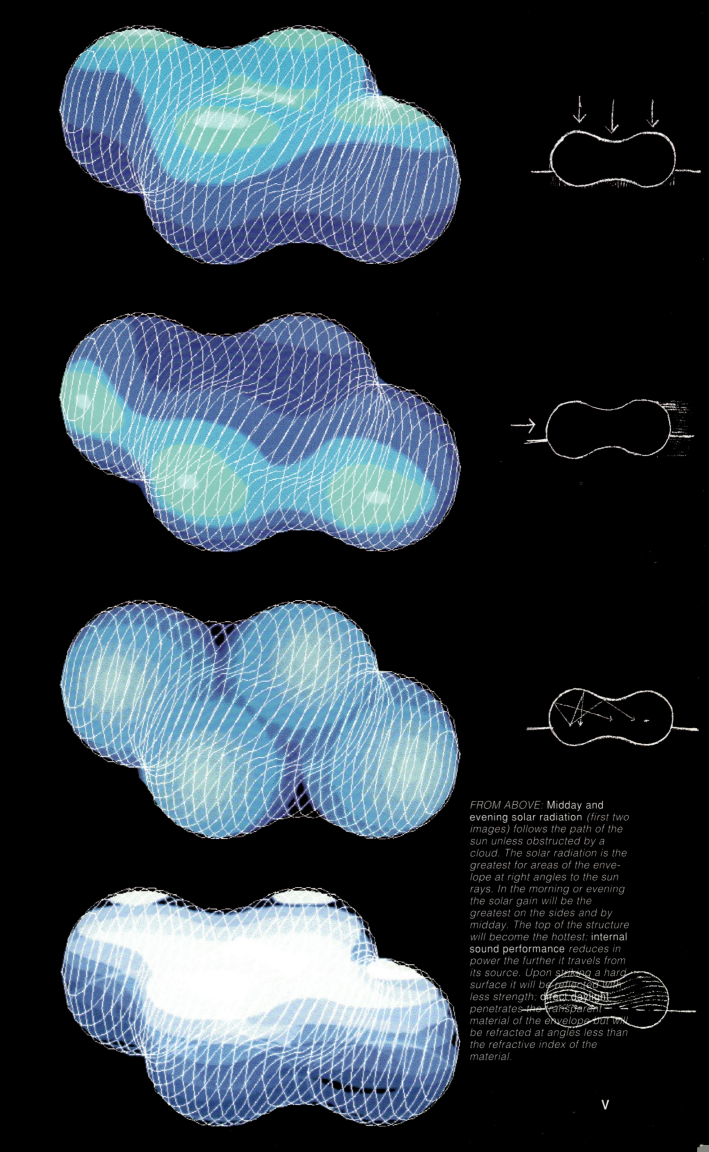

FROM ABOVE: Midday and evening solar radiation (first two images) follows the path of the sun unless obstructed by a cloud. The solar radiation is the greatest for areas of the envelope at right angles to the sun rays. In the morning or evening the solar gain will be the greatest on the sides and by midday. The top of the structure will become the hottest; internal sound performance reduces in power the further it travels from its source. Upon striking a hard surface it will be reflected with less strength; direct daylight penetrates the transparent material of the envelope but will be refracted at angles less than the refractive index of the material.

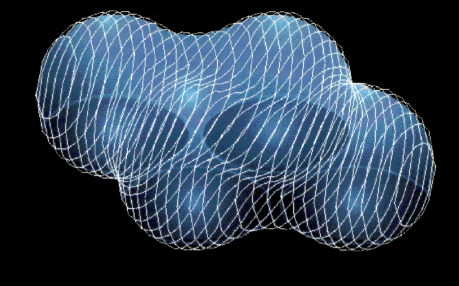

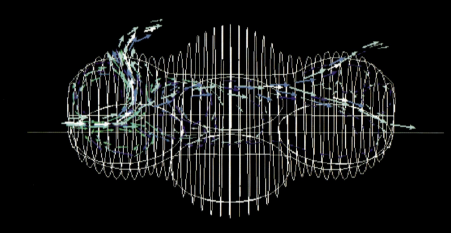

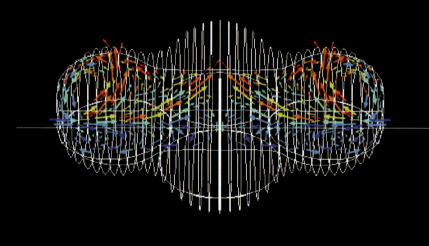

FROM ABOVE: Diffused skylight penetration will be determined by the aperture on view of the sky and therefore the majority of the light will penetrate through horizontal elements; **air circulation due to wind pressure differential**: *as the wind speed increases around the profile of an obstruction, the pressure drops. Low pressure draws in air molecules to reinstate equilibrium, creating a draught;* **air circulation due to thermal pressure differential**: *as air temperature rises the density drops and becomes buoyant compared with cooler air around it. With the air molecules growing further apart the density is reduced and therefore it rises. As the air cools down, the density increases and sinks; thus generating a cycle of air movement;* **nighttime re-radiation**: *on clear nights the building envelope will radiate heat to the outer atmosphere. Exposed areas to atmosphere elements will radiate at a greater rate than vertical elements. The sea water, due to its thermal mass, will remain warmer than the cooling structure and will warm the soffit of the structure.*

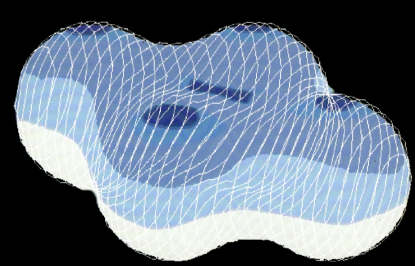

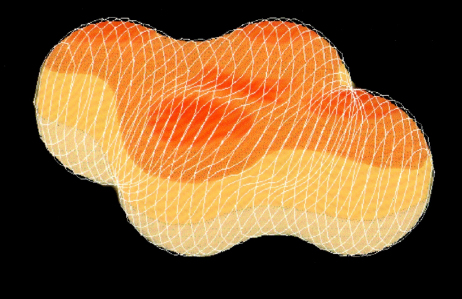
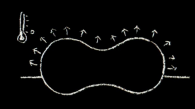

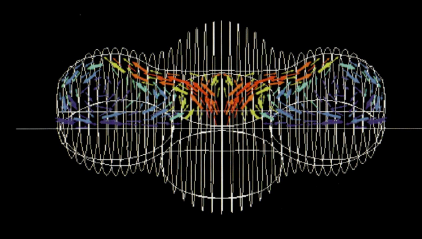
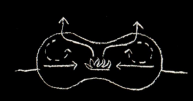

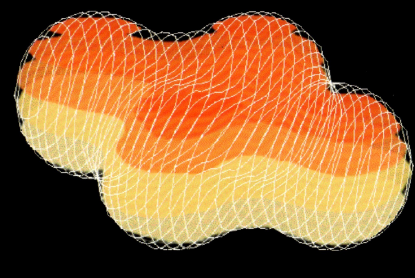
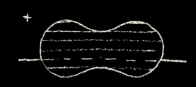

FROM ABOVE: **Radiation heat loss in the winter** *on a still day will increase with height as the thermal differential beteen inside and out rises;* **fire and smoke escape:** *a fire is a source of intense heat which lowers the density of the air, which then lifts, taking with it the dust particles of burnt material. As it cools, the density increases and it proceeds to fall;* **thermal stratification** *is generated by the hot air being lighter than the heavier cool air. Heat loss will therefore increase with height as the thermal differential between inside and out increases;* **conventional heat loss during cold winds blowing** *will be the greatest on exposed faces and the least on sheltered areas.*

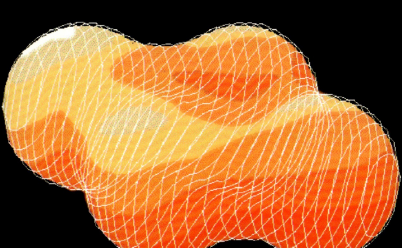

VII

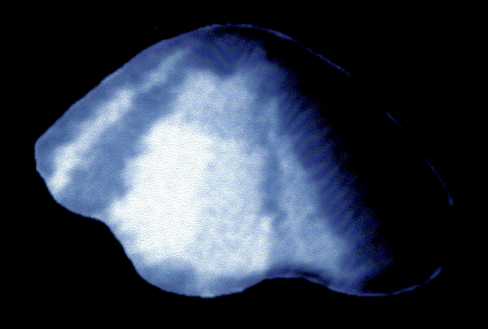

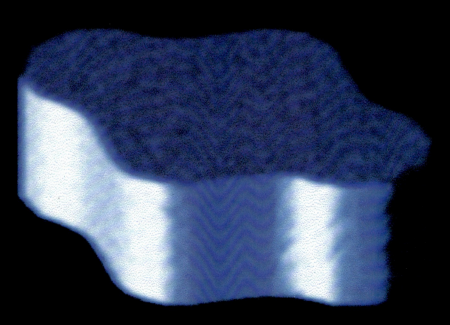

FROM ABOVE: Mechanical form; radiant form

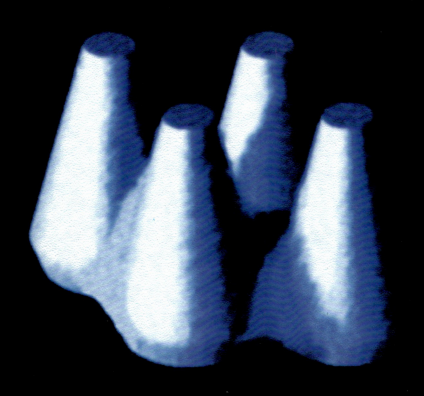

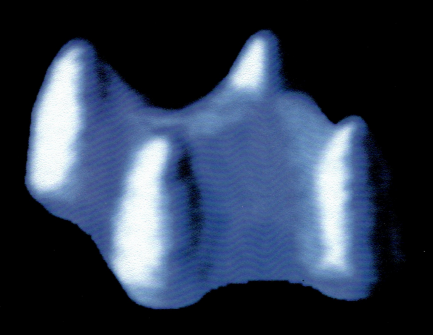

FROM ABOVE: Air molecular movement form; idealised form

GREEN BUILDINGS
OVE ARUP PARTNERSHIP

Like any colour, green can come in many shades. What is called 'green' today is likely to pale considerably by tomorrow's benchmarks. Fundamentally, 'Green Design' is not an identifiable objective but an attitude of mind. It means seeking to adapt our way of life to a more sustainable equilibrium with our fragile planet. This may eventually mean radical changes to how we live, but today for us as engineers it means that we must use our wit, our intellect and our innovative ability to develop technical solutions which work in greater harmony with our planet. This approach certainly involves a holistic attitude to problem-solving, addressing all the underlying issues. It also demands reappraisal of conventional solutions and standards.

Consider, for example, a green approach to an appropriate indoor environment. The conventional solution is to 'manufacture' a totally artificial climate out of 'Black boxes', with all the considerable energy and resources that involves. But the basic environmental needs of human beings can largely be met without these devices. Nature can be the prime provider, with mechanical systems giving secondary support. Thus most of the lighting can be by sunlight, cooling by ambient air and heating by human bodies and office equipment. These natural sources can be supplemented by other natural means: solar heating, ventilation driven by wind pressures and by solar buoyancy, cooling by water evaporation. These are ancient principles; modern computer-based methods of analysis and simulation enable us to understand them better and apply them with confidence.

Comfort criteria are another part of the story. Convention has it that we need 500 lux illumination and temperatures within a degree of 22 °C , even though this over-simplified approach does not reflect our full psychological and physiological needs. Air-conditioning systems may control air temperature but, because they do not recognise the full range of individual needs and expectations, too often they result in dissatisfied occupants. Today, comfort is being redefined to allow room temperatures that reflect daily and seasonal effects and which permit variations based on individual expectations combined with increased control over their local environment.

The third element in the green approach to the building environment is the building itself: its form, facade and materials. These act together as climate modifier, smoothing and redirecting the fluctuations of nature. Thus the external wall can capture daylight and transmit it to the inside. It can protect against excess glare, provide shading, ventilation air and cooling ability. It contains internal heat in winter and it provides visual contact with the world outside. Within the building, air movement can be directed by roof form, thermal flues, and atria controlled by louvred openings. The buildings that come from this approach tend to be simpler and more integrated. Internal conditions tend to be more stable, remaining moderate even at extremes of outdoor temperature. They have more flexibility. Should future circumstances demand it, a passively-cooled, naturally-ventilated building can usually have air-conditioning added, but the converse is rarely possible. Capital costs can be reduced. Running costs are less, energy consumption and pollution emissions are lower, and the sue of non-sustainable resources is reduced. Occupants have more control; they are less at the mercy of machinery, the environment is more human and – the real objective – they feel more comfortable.

Examples of green building philosophies in practice can be seen in the 22-storey Austrian Cultural Centre in New York City. Designed by Atelier Raimund Abraham, this building uses solar panels, heat pumps, high insulation standards and occupancy and daylight sensors to create an energy-efficient environment.

The Cable & Wireless training facility in Coventry designed by MacCormac Jamieson Prichard uses the wave form of the teaching room roofs to generate buoyancy-driven cross-ventilation sufficient to remove the high internal heat gains generated by information technology equipment.

The Inland Revenue Centre in Nottingham, designed by Michael Hopkins and Partners, provides 40000 m² of naturally ventilated office and ancillary accommodation for completion in late 1994. Its highly integrated architectural, structural and environmental form gives excellent delighting, solar shading and thermal flywheel abilities. Glazed stair towers provide solar and wind assistance to natural ventilation. The project is the first to gain maximum points under the

Royal Hong Kong Jockey Club clubhouse; OPPOSITE: Austrian Cultural Centre in New York City

XII

Building Research Establishment Environmental Assessment Method.

The five-storey computer department at the University of Northumbria, Newcastle is the first building in the UK to be clad in photovoltaic cells which generate electricity from sunlight. It is part of a £1.5m refurbishment being carried out by a consortium whose members include Arups, Newcastle Photovoltaics Centre, BP Solar and IT Power.

National University of Science and Technology, Zimbabwe designed by Davis Brody & Associates with Tibbalds Monro and Mwamuka Mercuri Associates, has a relatively mild climate but high levels of solar radiation. By developing a structural slab system with optimal thermal mass characteristics and by using a variety of shading devices, mechanical heating and cooling are eliminated in virtually all parts of this major development.

The GSW Headquarters building in Berlin designed by Sauerbruch & Hutton is a 23-storey tower block linked to the 1950s building. A double facade on the west elevation creates thermal flues and induces natural ventilation, thereby eliminating any need for air-conditioning.

The brief for the new 6000 m² Learning Resource Centre for Anglia Polytechnic University, currently on site in Essex, called for an environmentally-conscious, low-energy building. In a design by the ECD Partnership, the key elements involve an integrated approach using natural ventilation and exposed high thermal capacity structure. Daylighting at the perimeter is maximised by the window design which incorporates twin internal light shelves. Artificial lighting and opening windows are controlled from the central computer.

Düsseldorfer Stadttor designed by Ingenhoven Overdiek & Petzinka, is a speculative 18-floor, 3,2000 m² office development in the centre of Düsseldorf. The building has a full height glazed, naturally-ventilated double facade consisting of single glazed external cladding, reflective blinds and internal double glazing.

The extensive facilities of the Royal Hong Kong Jockey Club clubhouse designed by the architects Robert Matthew Johnson Marshall, carry with them heavy energy demands, especially for heating. Four heating systems are available and the most efficient to suit prevailing conditions is selected automatically.

Excerpt from *Arup Focus* 1/1994

FROM ABOVE: Inland Revenue Centre, Nottingham; National University of Science and Technology, Zimbabwe; Anglia Polytechnic University, Essex; LEFT: University of Northumbria, Newcastle; OPPOSITE, FROM ABOVE: Cable & Wireless training facility in Coventry; GSW Headquarters in Berlin

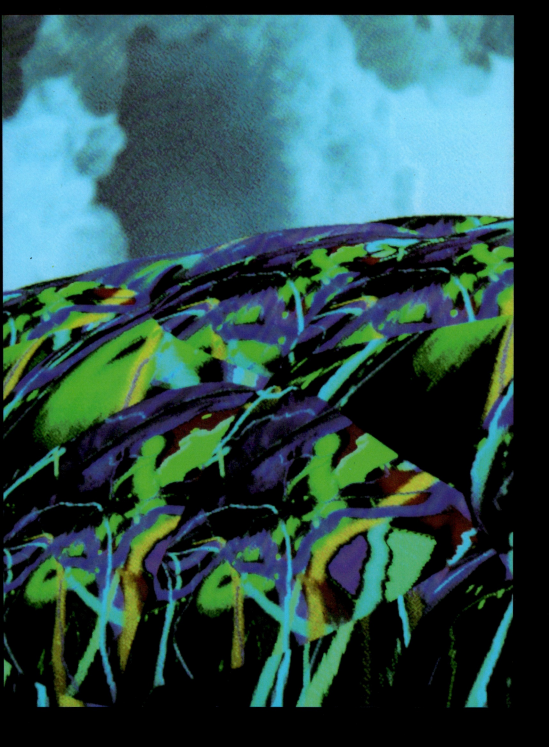

WHEN IS A DOOR NOT A DOOR?
NEIL SPILLER

Our self-satisfied attitude to the inertia of our buildings is becoming untenable. Architects building for the 21st century will have to smarten up. The idea that a new building must respect any urban context will become spurious faced with an architecture of motility. The purpose of this article is to swiftly chart the search for biological mimics and vitalistic architecture; to point out the ground breaking advances in smart material research and to guess some philosophical issues that may emerge.

Once architecture becomes buildable we are compromised by the ignorance of our materials. We have been conditioned by some foolish ideas about building buildings. Consider the brick, its merits, we are told, are its variety of colours, its human scale, its simple jointing methods and its procurement advantages; in fact its merits do not include a capacity to keep water out. The use of brick in building necessitates many preventative methods including damp proof courses and even the provision of another wall 75mm behind to stop water travelling to the inner face and allow space for insulation; a house within a house – a silly idea for the end of the 20th century.

One of the reasons for the proliferation of so called 'paper' architects is the inertia of the materiality of building compared to the dynamic of architectural theory and an ever evolving culture.

Perhaps, before describing two aspects of current technological theory, it might be beneficial to trace the infatuation man has had in trying to mimic biological systems. Some of the first recorded attempts involve the creation of automata. In the third century BC, a craftsman called Yen Shuh is supposed to have invented a mechanical man. This is the first record of the human quest to construct facsimiles of ourselves. Automata have a rich and surreal past. They become analogous to man's search for a mechanistic universe. Stories abound such as the tale of Jacques Vaucanson, who if the hand bills are to be believed, invented life in the guise of a mechanical duck which drank, ate, quacked, splashed about in water and even deposited duck droppings. The Japanese, who would sometimes refer to themselves as the *robotto okaku* (the kingdom of robots), have a distinguished history of automata research dating from the mid 16th century, including erotic automata for hire during the mid 1600s.

In alchemy automata have been used to symbolise man's reconciled existence within nature.

Some alchemic texts talk of the homunculus, an artificial man. The great alchemist philosopher Paracelsus wrote that the beginning of the process for creation of the homunculus is to develop a concoction which includes human semen. It is clear that by this time the creation of human facsimilies was seen, by the alchemists at least, as presenting special issues in relation to man and his integration with nature. The alchemists' homunculus was not intended to be mechanical but biological in some way. They were not interested in cogs, gears and so on but a state of oneness between man and his universe, whether that universe was cosmological or microscopic in scale.

In architecture during the 21st century, biological motifs and forms have been used, as they have in previous centuries, to symbolise an architecture close to and inspired by nature. This practice continued through Art Nouveau via the Bowellist adventures of the 1960s to the search for isotropic space and the movable pod idea, which still exists – all these notions were limited by inert materials.

The quest for biologically informed constructions, whether architecture or artificial intelligence, has a long and mixed history. It has been well known by some that intelligent materials, when they came, would totally alter our understanding of the word 'building' and have a far reaching effect on the human condition. We are on the threshold of this. Function will not be linked to materiality to the extent that it is now. The problem of mimicking large scale biological elements by purely mechanical means has forced experiments to adopt a microscopic scale. It is at this scale that truly responsive systems have to be developed, but adaptations and motions are impossible to control. Perhaps this blockage of thinking has been caused in part by the belief in a mechanised universe. Until recently, advances in material science had been conditioned by hard engineering to developing materials that rejoice in their capacity for inertia: low expansion; low

Spiller Farmer research project, 1993; OPPOSITE: *Nigel Greenhill,* Smart Skin

contraction; high impermeability – creating specific materials for different jobs whilst not recognising the multivalence of the biotic sphere as a worthy field of research.

Two recent breakthroughs in smart material technology, will prove to be crucial to architecture, these are Polymer Gels and Nano-Technology. Polymer Gels are less dramatic but definitely important in their consequence. The building industry likes to avoid 'wet' trades; however, in the future all building may well be wet. Gels consist of a series of long polymer molecules and a liquid. The molecular make-up of the liquid, or solvent as it is called, can cause the polymer molecules to expand or contract in a muscular way. Reactions can be caused by varying the levels of pH, intensity of an electric field or temperature, depending on the use of different types of gel and solvents. These gels could be the start of self-sensing and self-regulating 'soft' machines. Experiments have already been successfully conducted that have had gels striking small balls (gel golf or gelf), and edging along a rachetted beam.

The second and perhaps most astounding theoretical development in materials is that of Nano-technology. 'Nano' relies on the, at first amazing yet theoretically possible, idea of developing molecular sized 'factories' (replicators) that would include components such as assemblers, tape readers, chemical processors and a simple computer. In total, these replicator parts would number one billion atoms and be able to self copy itself in 15 minutes, the same rate as bacteria. At the end of ten hours of replicating, 68 billion nano machines could be developed, as the growth would be exponential. These machines could then be used to assemble or reassemble molecular structures, capable of developing any form of molecular arrangement and therefore any material. Each material will then have the ability to transform into any other, providing the raw material atoms are present. This process of raw material provision would be enabled by either growing materials in vats or ducting them in liquid form to the replicators. It is possible to grow anything in a vat – a rocket engine perhaps!

These chemomechanical systems could herald the dawn of super-smart materials: 'Wetware'. Leaving aside the obvious potential of Nano-technology for rejuvenating the ill and indeed the dead, what does this mean for architecture? It could mean that designs for building will replicate. A building might have a mother, or owners or users could grow new book shelves, floors or walls. Obviously in a nano-building the air would always be fresh. Architecture would be responsive like never before; it might even disappear. Honeymoon couples could grow a new home whilst sunning themselves on a foreign shore, providing a neighbour made sure it did not dry up. Buildings would become conscious – alive. Descartes 'cogito ergo sum' translated by Spinoza as 'I am conscious, therefore I exist' becomes important in relation to the built fabric of our cities. It has recently been said that some apes have the intelligence of a two-year-old child and therefore should be given human rights. In time, buildings will become more intelligent than this: should buildings be given human rights? What of demolition without the building's permission. Is this murder? Or indeed with its permission, is this euthanasia? Perhaps what is needed is a series of laws akin to Assimov's Laws of Robotics which focus around protecting humans, obeying humans and protecting the self in that order of priority. This huge philosophical debate is one that is happening in the scientific community, particularly in reference to Artificial Intelligence, but not in architecture. Architects must research these avenues as architecture is where the philosophical issues of the 'aliveness' of smart materials will become paramount.

Living in a house is not the same as living with your home. When is a door not a door? When it is called Brenda and it is good enough to eat by its own light.

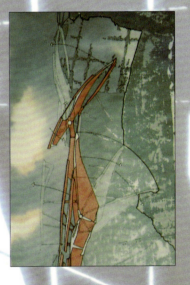

Images from Spiller Farmer research project 1993

news *competition*

A MINIMALIST SOLUTION
Dido Milne and Tom Russell

King's College Chapel is Cambridge's most celebrated landmark. It attracts as many as 1,000 visitors per hour over the summer months. A limited competition was organised in order to develop ideas of a permanent facility for visitors to the college; the winners were architectural students at the university, Dido Milne and Tom Russell.

They chose a minimalist solution using two basic elements: a shallow pool that runs parallel to the chapel and a deep wall within which the gift shop is located.

The gift shop is enclosed along its length by two parallel stone walls. By freeing these walls' front indicators of scale, such as door and window openings, they will read from both sides as garden walls, thereby avoiding the problem of the scale of the intervention and its relationship with the adjoining chapel. A smaller wall runs perpendicular to the shop protruding slightly from the line of the chapel to indicate the entrance. The end wall of the building is glazed, allowing visitors within the shop to look out through the loggia attached to the front of the Old Schools to Caius College *Gate of Honour*.

The pool marks a route to the chapel and a boundary between the Old Schools. It serves as a trough collecting rainwater and its shape emphasises the linearity of the space. The rhythm of the chapel's down pipes is picked up in gutters inlaid across the path.

The final understatement concerns the texture of the wall facing the chapel. Its surface responds to that of the chapel but at sunset the play of light from the adjacent pool and the reflections of the overhanging branches of the horse-chesnut tree dissolve the materiality of the stone.

news exhibitions

PLASTICS

'Soft, hard, flexible, thin, light, opaque, transparent, translucent, elastic, rigid, in the form of foam, film, gel or an alloy' – the development of the polymeric material PLASTIC was one of the great technological achievements of the past hundred years. Although plastics have beome ubiquitous in late 20th-century life, largely through ignorance, our attitude towards them remains ambivalent.

In the 19th century, plastics were considered beautiful and aspirational – capable of make-believe promises of tortoiseshell, ivory and horn. In the inter-war years their utopian qualities were promoted. Bakelite was used for new gadgets such as wirelesses and radios. However mass produced plastics in America meant that plastics came to symbolise all that was inferior, cheap and tacky. In the 50s, architects and designers used them to embody ideas of the modern movement while in the 60s their expandability, new textures and colours made them the LSD of materials. In the 70s the reputation of plastics was soured as toxic pollutants derived from plastics became an environmental nightmare. In the 80s and 90s they have re-emerged as a socially, environmentally and even sexually responsible substance. Their rehabilitaion has been encouraged by their expanding role within medical and space research and the invention of biodegradable plastics.

From October '94 to April '95 the PLASTICS exhibition at the Design Museum in London will address the social, economic, environmental and cultural values of plastics. The variety of plastics to be studied will stretch from plastic used at the breakfast table to that designed for use in a nuclear fall-out shelter, analysing those plastics used in industry, medicine, fashion and communications on the way.

The implications of plastic for the future of architecture are enormous. Jan Kaplicky of the progressive architectural firm, Future Systems, predicts that plastics are the way forward. The Finnish Neste Corporation embarked on the Nestehaus project in Scandanavia in the 70s to demonstrate how extensively plastic might be incorporated into both non-structural and structural elements of a two-storey house. Plastics were found to solve major problems posed by chemical corrosion and electroconductivity. Combined with wood, metal and concrete, they increase strength and durability of these traditional building materials. The are already extensively used for non-structural roles such as PVC piping, vinyl windows and siding, and plastic foam insulation. Limited application of plastics for structural or load-bearing purposes is mostly due to the prohibitive cost of fibreglass-reinforced plastic beams and reinforcing bar and panels formed in a process called 'pultrusion'. The potential of plastics in architecture will be addressed by Christopher McCarthy and Guy Battle in the next issue of *Architectural Design*.

FROM ABOVE: LM Ericsson, Sweden 1931, Telephone set; Fundator, Sweden 1950-60s, Cups and saucers

XIX

reviews books

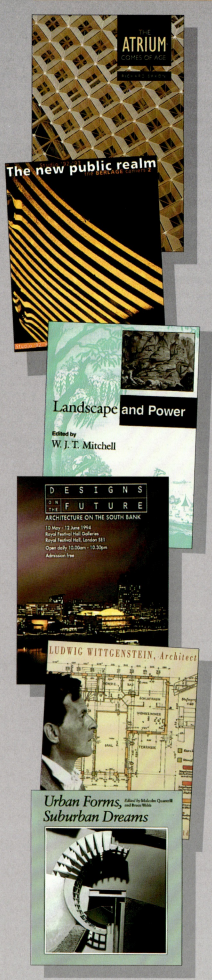

THE ATRIUM COMES OF AGE by Richard Saxon, Longman Group, 1994, 120pp, colour ills, HB £55
The atrium, in its modern enclosed form, dates back 200 years. It re-emerged as a favoured design concept in north America in the late 1960s in the form of large-scale glazed volumes for both public and private use. However it was not until the 1980s that atrium building gained world-wide popularity, with the initiative and innovation in design and technology passing to Europe and Japan.

Richard Saxon introduces the subject by examining the 'prehistory' of the modern atrium: the Dome, Brighton 1806 by Richard Porden; Garage Marbeuf, Paris 1929 by Laprade and Bazin and the Peabody Library, Baltimore 1878 by EG Lind. These buildings influenced the commercial buildings, where in some cases atrium space was given priority over rentable floor space. Examples include IM Pei's notorious glass pyramid, the rooflight to the central atrium of the new public entrance.

This book also provides valuable practical information on issues such as fire safety in atruim buildings, using research from the United States, United Staates, United Kingdom and Japan.

THE NEW PUBLIC REALM The Berlage cahiers 2, Studio '92-'93, 010 Publishers, Rotterdam, 1994, 100pp, colour ills, PB, price NA
One of the most interesting projects that the students of the Berlage Insitute focus on in this anthology of their year's work is Media Culture. The results of their investigation into the impact of media on contemporary design are imaginative and innovative. They work from the premise that 'from large cinematic cultural centres to small fair pavilions and exhibition installations, a non-phenomenological approach has been taken in order to recognise and analyse the essence of the immaterial, the media, the message and the image as a design pedagogy. Today the relationship between man and his environment has become defined more by the 'visual' (ie image, sound and colour) rather than by the 'tactile'. Student solutions include Evert Crols and Vasa Perovic's 'Electronic Territories', a mega cinema in an industrial landscape and 'Lying Obelisk' by Mikio Tai. Another section focuses on the evaluation of architecture to improve the ability of one to criticise in a constructive way. Ignasi de Sola Morales claimed that 'architecture is a network. Empiricism of fact is the only way to find out what architecture is. The final aim of criticism is to understand the present time'.

LANDSCAPE AND POWER edited by WJT Mitchell, University of Chicago Press, 1994, 248pp, b/w ills, PB £11.25, Cloth £33.95
Landscapes, whether in pictures or the world, have been viewed as a genre, treated as texts, interpreted as allegory. In the opening essay, Mitchell examines the ways in which the concept of landscape functions in the discourse of imperialism, from Chinese imperial landscape to views of contested territory in New Zealand and Israel. Essays by Ann Jensen Adams, Ann Vermingham, Elizabeth Helsinger, David Bunn, Joel Snyder and Charles Harrison, range from Dutch landscape and the formation of national identity to picturesque landscape and the process of political silencing and legitimating. Other topics include Turner's tourist landscapes as reflections on the conditions of political representation, American landscape photography and the professionalising of the frontier, domestic British landscapes transferred to South Africa in the 19th century and forms of resistance to ideology in modernist landscape painting.

DESIGNS ON THE FUTURE Architecture on the South Bank, Hugh Pearman, The South Bank and the Architecture Foundation, 15pp, colour ills, price NA
Hugh Pearman traces the history of this area of the South Bank of the Thames in London from its pre-war warehouses through the Festival of Britain constructed on the bombed site in the 1950s up to the present day. This area is home to prestigious national and international corporations and to Europe's largest centre for the arts and media and a growing residential population. With the opening of Waterloo International it becomes London's gateway to Europe. However it is often perceived as a bleak and hostile area, lacking shops and street level activity and difficult for pedestrians to navigate. A symposium in June, organised by the South Bank Centre and the Academy Group Ltd, brought together a cross section of important architectural minds, such as Zaha Hadid and Nigel Coates, to respond to 'Designing the Future of the South Bank'.

LUDWIG WITTGENSTEIN, Architect by Paul Wijdeveld, Thames and Hudson, 300pp, colour ills, HB £45
The compelling power of Ludwig Wittgenstein's genius, which changed the course of Western philosophy, emerged unmistakably in everything he executed. Between 1926 and 1928, in partnership with the architect Paul Englemann, he designed and built a house – the Kundmanngasse – in Vienna for his sister Margaret Stonborough. Although Englemann was an experienced architect and former pupil of Adolf Loos, Wittgenstein dominated the collaboration and is credited with the design which emerged as a uniquely unified, elegant and austere example of early architectural Modernism. This book describes the philosopher's temporary assumption of the status of the architect, his ideas about aesthetics in general and architecture in particular, as well as his obsessive quest for 'functionalism, perfectionism and elegance as a consequence of truthfulness in thinking and acting'.

URBAN FORMS, SUBURBAN DREAMS edited by Malcom Quantrill and Bruce Webb, Texas A&M University Press, 162pp, b/w ills, HB $50
One of the primary tasks for architecture in today's world is to create a sense of place for the contemporary community – meshing urban density with suburban growth and change is 'neither here nor there'. Both urb (city) and suburb in our society challenge architects to conceive through social engineering and geometric design a sense of wonder in space. Peter Eisenman proposes that the media, tele-video especially, have dissolved all distinctions between the 'here and there,' one place and another. Colin Rowe on the other

reviews books

hand sees the city as a distinct 'place' if different from the modernist formula vision. He believes it is a collage that can best be understood as a three-dimensional jigsaw puzzle. Kaisa Broner-Bauer's account traces the modern movement's idealism to its 19th century precursors and raises the question of what happened to the planners of the brave new world in fascist Italy.

BOUNDARIES OF THE CITY The Architecture of Western Urbanism by Alan Waterhouse, University of Toronto Press, 342pp, b/w ills, HB, price NA
In this study Alan Waterhouse draws on anthropology, social and cultural history, literature, and philosophy to reach an understanding of the roots of Western architecture and city building. He explores the illusion that cities are constructed to impose rational order, an order articulated through urban boundaries. These boundaries are shaped around our instinctive fears and insecurities about crime, insurrection, and the violent disruption of everyday life. At the same time, contrary instincts aspire to create a unified domain, to proclaim the interdependence of things through constructed work. Cities are shaped less by rational design than by a recurring dialectic of boundary formation. These impulses underlie the formal vocabulary of architecture and urbanism.

THE KLOSTERKIRCHHOF HOME by Júrgen Baade and Diethelm Hoffman, Ernst & Sohn, 100pp, colour ills, PB, price NA
This carefully planned retirement home in Kiel, Germany, is designed to give the impression of dignified anonymity: the architects wanted to avoid any kind of enforced cosiness and were at pains to make private and semi-public areas distinct.

The Klosterkirchhof Home attempts to place old people at the centre of urban public life and allows them to withdraw into a private environment which would normally have no place in this part of the city. The emphasis on individuality and on encouraging and personal interpretation of private space has evolved into a design which is conducive to retired life.

The circulation spaces have an air of sobriety lit by relatively impersonal industrial lights in striking contrast to the elegant circular light fittings next to the doors. Daylight penetrates every corner of the building as a result of the extensive use of glass panels and the glazed roof light in the attic.

FACADISM by Jonathan Richards, Routledge, 170pp, b/w ills, HB, price NA
The controversy surrounding facadism began in Britain but surfaced throughout the West in the 1980s with the massive investment in urban redevelopment. Development decisions are made through the interaction of a variety of interests. Central government, local planning authorities, developers, architects, clients and amenity pressure groups have very different ways of valuing aesthetics, conservation, innovation and cost.

Britain provides ample examples of an historical impulse towards ordered, dignified and sometimes beautiful settings of urban living. Facadism questions the value of such a past in our present. Are we concerned with a conservation principle within which street elevations are paramount, an architectural philosophy which designs buildings round facades; a marketing technique which combines heritage planning with the increasing demands on the built environment, or the very concept of what constitutes urban identity?

DROTTNINGHOLM COURT THEATRE Its Advent, Fate and Preservation, edited by Ove Hidemark, Per Eström, Birgitta Schyberg et al, 142pp, colour ills, PB, price NA
Skärva, a fascinating architectural experiment done in the 1780s in classical and Swedish vernacular styles, is a small country house by the Baltic in southern Sweden. Its owner, Fredrick af Chapman, the celebrated naval architect, and his friend and official superior, Admiral Carl August Ehrensvärd, collaborated on its design. Its classical elements are by Ehrensvärd, and its nautical elements by Chapman.

The 18th-century theatre building, together with the palace premises as a whole and the park, has been classified by UNESCO as one of the most valuable building complexes in the world. For music lovers all over the world, the name of Drottningholm Court Theatre resounds with the same magic as that of Stradivarius since large number of the instruments that Stradivarius built between 1666 and 1737 are still used by the contemporary violinists.

ARCHITECTS HOUSE THEMSELVES by Michael Webb, The Preservation Press, Washington, 223pp, colour ills, HB $39.95
Ever since Thomas Jefferson built Monticello, American architects have used their own houses as laboratories, testing new ideas and putting a fresh spin on the old. Pioneers like Schindler, Neutra, Wright, Gropius, Charles and Ray Eames and Philip Johnson explored new ways of enclosing space and relating buildings to nature. They shocked their contemporaries and inspired their successors. The latest work shown here ranges from a tree house in Berkeley to a playful weekend cottage on Lake Michigan; from a cluster of wooden towers in a Florida palm grove to a Toronto house that fuses craft and technology. Sophisticated New York apartments, daring hillside houses in LA and witty variations on the New England vernacular reflect America's regional diversity.

SOCRATES' ANCESTOR An Essay on Architectural Beginnings by Indra Kagis McEwen, MIT Press, 194pp, b/w ills, PB £13.50, Cloth £26.95
'If architecture is concerned with order, its omnipresent origins must be told in connection with the history of philosophy'. McEwen argues that it was here in the archaic Greek polis, that Western architecture became the cradle of Western thought. He analyses the period in detail, even concentrating on tools such as the 'gnomon' similar to a set square. Rather like a sundial, he argues that it is an emblem of the exactitude required for proper interpretation of signs emitted from a divine source.

McEwen's appreciation of the early Greek understanding of the indissolubility of craft and community yields new insight into such issues as orthogonal planning and the appearance of the encompassing colonnade, the ptera, or wings that made Greek temples Greek.

XXI

reviews books

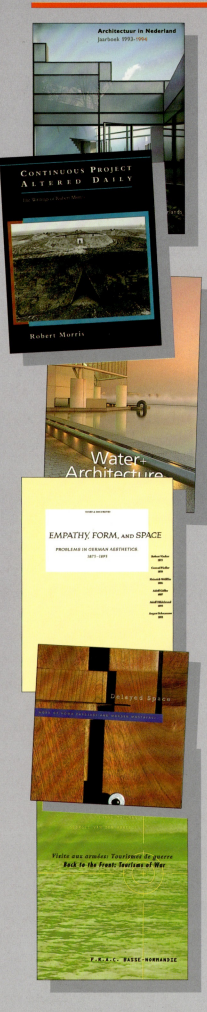

Who was Socrates' ancestor? Socrates claims that it was Daedalus, the mythical first architect. McEwen draws out the connections between Daedalus and the earliest Greek thinkers, between architecture and the advent of speculative thought.

ARCHITECTURE OF THE NETHERLANDS Yearbook 1993-1994, 184pp, colour ills, PB, Nlg 75
This book consists of a selection of buildings which have been completed in the past year. It shows that the average level is high in the field of housing in the Netherlands. An essay on 'Modern Architecture of the 1950s and 60s' addresses this 'post heroic' era. Modernistic concepts converged with traditionalistic ones and were stripped of their social reforming ideals in order to ultimately arrive in the 1960s at an international standardised modernism. The buildings of an entire generation of architects from the 1950s and 60s are silently disappearing through demolition or drastic renovations. Also striking is how interior designers apparently harassed by architecture on the one side and designers on the other, have found new opportunities in the rapidly changing use of buildings. New architecture in the Netherlands has many faces. A considered selection of 22 works by Wiel Arets, Ben van Berkel, Herman Hertzberger, Liesbeth van der Pol, Frank and Paul Wintermans, Benthem Crouwel, DKV, Mecanoo, Mart van Schijndel, Baneke Van der Hoeven, Claus and Kaan, Cees Nagelkerke, Rudy Uytenhaak, Charles Vandenhove, Kees Christiaanse, Karelse Van der Meer, Jo Coenen, Siza/Geurst and Schulze.

CONTINUOUS PROJECT ALTERED DAILY The Writings of Robert Morris by Robert Morris, MIT Press, 330pp, b/w ills, HB £40.50
Robert Morris is best known for his significant contributions to minimalist sculpture and antiform art, as well as for a number of widely influential theoretical writings on art. Illustrated throughout, this collection of his seminal essays from the 1960-80 addresses wide-ranging intellectual and philosophical problems of sculpture, raising issues of materiality, size and shape, anti-illusionism, and perceptual conditions. Included are the influential 'Notes on Sculpture' which carefully articulates the shifting terrains of sculpture during the 1960s, tracing its movement from the gestalt-driven unitary forms of minimalism, through permutable pieces, to the formally dispersed process-oriented antiform art that appeared later in the decade, and Morris's landmark essay, 'Anti Form' which marked a departure from art as object.

WATER + ARCHITECTURE by Charles W Moore and Jane Lidz, Thames and Hudson, 224pp, colour ills, HB £36
Architecture engages in a continual dialogue with its environment and water is one of the fundamental elements of that dialogue. Water as an architectural resource has featured ever since the first architecture was created, in all kinds of ways: but never until now has it been the subject of a systematic study. The collaboration between Charles Moore and Jane Lidz covers styles ranging from classical to post-modern, building types encompass humble plazas to palaces, sites from across Europe, the United States, China, Japan and South-East Asia. Famous examples range from the Trevi Fountain in Rome to the great torii gate at Miyajima in Japan. The symbolism of water as a design elements is analysed alongside specific applications in all kinds of structures and settings: fountains and waterfalls, rivers and canals, lakes and pools, oceans and islands.

EMPATHY, FORM AND SPACE, Problems in German Aesthetics 1873-1893, introduction by Harry Francis Mallgrave and Eleftherios Ikonomou, The Getty Centre, 330pp, PB £19.95, Cloth £39.95
The six essays presented in this volume afford the English-reading public the first serious and considered overview of the uniquely Germanic movements of psychological aesthetics and Kunstwissenschaft. Written in the last three decades of the 19th century – at a time when the proliferation of knowledge and dramatic social and economic change had combined to force the issue of art's exhaustion of its traditional historical themes – these seminal writings helped to redesign the theoretical foundation of modern artistic practice. The earlier metaphysical problem of how we structure and understand form and space in the natural world, in essence gave way to the aesthetic problem of how we might appreciate and actually exploit pure form and pure space artistically in painting, sculpture, music as well as architecture.

DELAYED SPACE by Homa Fardjadi and Mohsen Mostafavi, Harvard University Graduate School of Design, 145pp, colour ills, PB, price NA
This monograph presents recent work by architects Homa Fardjadi and Mohsen Mostafavi. The current trend in both architectural practice and criticism toward extremities in theory has in some circles ruled out a discussion of actual buildings. Excluded from such discourse is the 'middle ground' of architecture: the space of the building itself. The work of Homa Fardjadi and Mohsen Mostafavi forces a reconsideration of this middle ground as more than the site of daily functioning but as 'that which instigates the activities it also contains and presents'.

BACK TO THE FRONT: TOURISM OF WAR by Diller + Scofidio, Princeton Architectural Press, 328pp, b/w and colour ills, PB, price NA
Diller + Scofidio are atypical architects: they do not regard architectural production as a means of perpetuating and consolidating society, of an evolution towards utopia. Rather they see it as a tool for reading and interpreting what exists, and what is 'recorded or pre-recorded'. Their approach is no doubt descriptive but it is aimed at dismantling the mechanisms that govern our thinking and our behaviour. In their introduction they analyse the etymology of the word travel which derives from 'travail' to conclude that travel is linked to aggression. Thus tourism and war, which appear to be polar extremes of cultural activity, are technically linked. Israel is taken as an example of the symbiosis between tourism and war where the Gross National Product is largely depend-

reviews books

ent on a tourist industry and a large percentage of that money is spent directly on defence. So 'war is fuelled by tourism within war'.

INDUSTRIAL DESIGN by Christian Marquart, Ernst & Sohn, 308pp, b/w ills, HB, price NA

Our civilisation consists of a universe of things. It is crammed full of devices from countless periods and cultures. A homogenous world of objects emerges only where life itself is reduced to a few functions, such as prestigious rituals. The uniform lifestyle that the Bauhaus artists still had in mind, an everyday world consistently shaped in aesthetic terms from the coffee cup to the city as a casing for human life, is no longer on the agenda since the days of Post-Modernism with its pluralist positions. Instead of continuing to strive for uniformity, we have accepted and nourished pluralism in design. The main section of the book is concerned with the work of Hans Theo Baumann, Karl Dittert, Herbert Hirche, Günter Kupetz, Peter Raacke, Rainer Schütze, Hans Erich Slany and Arno Votteler, the fathers of the Verband Deutscher Industrie-Designer, founded in Stuttgart in 1959.

HIROSHI HARA by Hiroshi Hara, GA Architect, 250pp, colour ills, PB, price NA

Hiroshi Hara conducted a series of research tours that led from the Mediterranean basin to Central and South America, Eastern Europe and the Middle East, India and Nepal, and finally to West Africa. In each place Hara applied his 'domain theory' which involved clarifying and cataloguing all that determines the physical pattern of a community. Latin American villages differed greatly from his expectations since he had a more coherent unit and instead found that even the borders of a village were not clearly defined. This global perspective characterises his eclectic style of architecture and sets the scene for the international pluralism of the future.

THEATRUM GEDANENSE, Fundacja Theatrum Gedanense Gdansk, 25pp, colour ills, PB, price NA

The ancient city of Gdansk in Poland will celebrate its millennium in 1997 by building a Renaissance theatre in the centre of the city. The Theatrum Gedanense Foundation aims to reconstruct the original playhouse which was built in the early seventeenth century. Although most 'Shakespearean' playhouses were polygonal, the theatre at Gdansk was based on the Fortune Theatre in London whose plan was square. The theatre will be reconstructed using pictorial evidence and the original builders contracts for the Fortune Theatre. The Theatrum Gedanense Foundation believes that the construction of the theatre will create a cultural centre of international importance and it has widespread support including the Prince of Wales, Sir Peter Hall, Andrzej Wadja and Günter Grass.

ANCIENT ARCHITECTS IL37, What Could the Ancient Master Builders have Invented? by Frei Otto, Institute for Lightweight Structures, 148 pages, colour ills, PB DM 37

The premise behind this book is that the history of architecture is primarily a history of ideas and inventions which were originated in the prehistoric period. The development of these ideas up to Antiquity has little documentation so it is difficult to evaluate them in the tradition of classical architectural history. A new approach has been developed at the Institute for Lightweight Structures (IL) under the direction of Frei Otto and it attempts to trace the path of ideas using experiments and re-invention. This book concentrates on the design and construction of houses and is split into three periods: the First Epoch, building only with hands; the Second Epoch, building with hands and hand tools and the Third Epoch, the high technology of Antiquity, comprising building with hands, tools and ancient machines. The use of 1,260 sketches and clear explanations of the process of development makes this book essential reading for architects, engineers and historians.

SEXUALITY & SPACE edited by Beatriz Colomina, Princeton Papers on Architecture, Princeton Architectural Press, 389 pages, b/w illus, PB $14.95

This book is the result of the 'Sexuality & Space' symposium held in 1990. It address the absence of the work of feminist theorists in architectural discourse and practice. In spite of a growing reciprocity in the exchange for ideas between contemporary critical theorists and architectural theorists, feminist works on representation, desire and the repression of sexuality have been ignored. The aim of the symposium and this book, which contains papers by Catherine Ingraham, Mark Wigley and Meaghan Morris, was not only to import work on sexuality into architectural discourse but set up an interdisciplinary exchange in which theories of sexuality are re-read in architectural terms and architecture is re-read in sexual terms.

NEW BRITISH ARCHITECTURE Twelve Young Design Practices Trained in Britain in the 1980's, The Architecture Foundation, 64pp, colour illus, PB £10

Published to coincide with the exhibition held at the Architecture Foundation in London during April and May 1994, this catalogue illustrates the work of the twelve selected design practices. Each practice was invited to submit one built work and a project in progress as well as designs for a specially commissioned house. The open brief, for a family house for four or five people not exceeding 200 metres square, has resulted in blueprints for our future domestic environment. Although varied in language and expression all put forward radical yet pragmatic solutions that could replace the construction techniques in this country with brighter, cheaper and visually stimulating spaces in which to live. This well produced catalogue with texts by Professor Robert Maxwell and John Welsh, editor of the RIBA Journal, provides evidence that the architects trained in the 1980's, practising in the 'lean and mean' 1990's, are committed to the continuation and reinterpretation of modern architecture.

ERRATA

Botond Bognar should have been credited for the photographs which accompanied the Symposium 'Learning from Tokyo' (page 8-17) in issue 1/2 Architectural Design, entitled 'Japanese Architecture III'. We apologise for this oversight.

XXIII

ACADEMY *highlights*

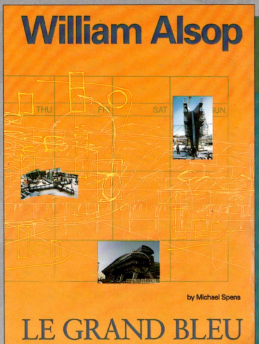

This fascinating study of Alsop and Störmer's building features the international award-winning competition scheme for the regional government offices in Marseilles. The building, completed in Spring 1994, has already been highly acclaimed in *Architectural Review*, *Building Design* and *Blueprint*. Illustrated throughout with design development drawings over three stages, the book also features Alsop's paintings which have stimulated his own ideas in progress. Working drawings, CAD drawings and detailed drawings of the innovative climate control complement the text, which describes in close detail the competition, the process of construction of this highly innovative building, and the complex as completed.

Hardback 1-85490-357 8
252 x 190 mm, 128 pages
174 illustrations, over 120 in colour
September 1994

Philippe Starck is an internationally known designer who is both a highly accomplished architect and also a designer of interior and industrial products. This is the first book to focus entirely on his architectural work which is much less well-known to the public. Thirty-seven projects in France, Japan, The United States, Italy, Spain and Germany will be featured including Paramount Hotel New York; Royalton Hotel New York, Cage Costen Pain; Nani Nani Building Tokyo; French pavilion Biennale Venice; Teatriz Restaurant Madrid.

Hardback 1-85490-378-0
280 x 256 mm (Portrait), 224 pages
over 200 illustrations, mostly in colour
September 1994

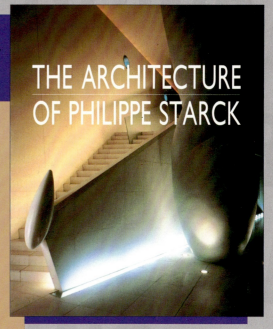

Further information can be obtained from Academy Group Ltd 071 402 2141

ASPECTS OF
MINIMAL ARCHITECTURE

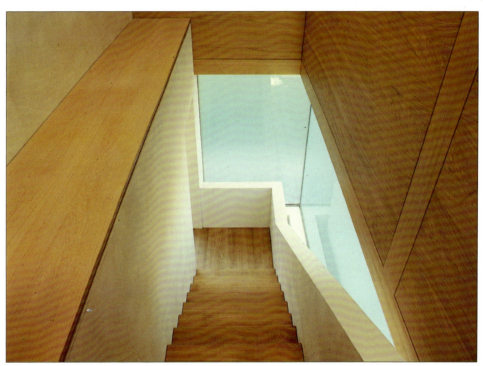

HERZOG & DE MEURON, GOETZ GALLERY, MUNICH, GERMANY

Architectural Design

ASPECTS OF
MINIMAL ARCHITECTURE

RICHARD MEIER & PARTNERS, ROYAL DUTCH PAPER MILLS HEADQUARTERS; *OPPOSITE*: CLAUDIO SILVESTRIN, JOHAN MENSWEAR SHOP, GRAZ, AUSTRIA; *OVERLEAF RIGHT*: JOHN PAWSON AND CLAUDIO SILVESTRIN, NEUENDORF HOUSE, MALLORCA, CONCEPTUAL SKETCH

ACADEMY EDITIONS · LONDON

Acknowledgements

We would like to thank The Chinati Foundation, Marfa, Texas and Donald Judd's family for supplying us with information following his recent death, and a particular mention to Claudio Silvestrin, Pierre d'Avoine, Tony Fretton, Trevor Horne, Terry Pawson and Keith Williams for their keen interest and ideas in this issue; also Duncan MacDonald and John Slaytor for their input. Extracts for the Legorreta essay were taken from *The Architecture of Ricardo Legorreta*, edited by Wayne Attoe assisted by Sydney H Brisker © 1990 University of Texas Press, 1990 Ernst & Sohn, Berlin.

Front Cover: Alberto Campo Baeza, Gaspar House, Zahora, Cadiz; *Inside Covers*: Katsuhiro Isobe, Landscaping Ring Zones, Amsterdam

Photographic Credits
All material is courtesy of the architects unless otherwise stated.
Franz Wimmer *pp1, 3, 59*; Scott Frances/Esto *pp3, 11, 50-57*; Hiroshi Ueda *pp6, 92-95*; Hisao Suzuki *Front Cover, pp8, 24-26, 27 centre*; Todd Eberle *pp9, 82-83*; Alberto Piovano/Arcaid *pp10, 30, 81*; Nathan Willock *p12*; Ian Dobbie *pp16, 64, 65 above*; Imanol Sistiaga *pp17, 66-67*; Jim Hedrich *p18 centre*; Armando Salas *p18 below*; Peter Aaron *p20 centre*; Colette Jauze *pp27 above and below, 28*; Pedro Albornoz *p31*; Chris Gascoigne *p43*; Eamonn O'Mahony *p44*; Philippe Ruault *pp46-49, 70-73*; Margherita Spiluttini *pp58, 60-61*; Richard Davies *pp62-63, 65 below*; Eduard Hueber *pp68-69*; Jan Derwig *p74 above*; Hans-Jürgen Commerell *p74 below*; Hélène Binet *p75*; Mark Pimlott *pp76-77*; Michael Moran *pp78-79*; Jeremy Cockayne/Arcaid *p80*; Katsuhisa Kida *pp84-86*; Kenji Kobayashi *p87*; Paul Warchol *p90*; Conrad Johnson *p91*; Tadao Ando *p95 below*

EDITOR: Maggie Toy
EDITORIAL TEAM: Iona Spens, Pip Vice, Katherine MacInnes
ART EDITOR: Andrea Bettella CHIEF DESIGNER: Mario Bettella
DESIGNER: Jan Richter

CONSULTANTS: Catherine Cooke, Terry Farrell, Kenneth Frampton, Charles Jencks
Heinrich Klotz, Leon Krier, Robert Maxwell, Demetri Porphyrios, Kenneth Powell, Colin Rowe, Derek Walker

First published in Great Britain in 1994 by *Architectural Design* an imprint of
ACADEMY GROUP LTD, 42 LEINSTER GARDENS, LONDON W2 3AN
Member of the VCH Publishing Group
ISBN: 1-85490-244-X (UK)

Copyright © 1994 the Academy Group Ltd *All rights reserved*
The entire contents of this publication are copyright and cannot be reproduced
in any manner whatsoever without written permission from the publishers

The Publishers and Editor do not hold themselves responsible for the opinions expressed by the
writers of articles or letters in this magazine
Copyright of articles and illustrations may belong to individual writers or artists
Architectural Design Profile 110 is published as part of *Architectural Design* Vol 64 7-8/1994
Architectural Design Magazine is published six times a year and is available by subscription

Distributed to the trade in the United States of America by
ST MARTIN'S PRESS, 175 FIFTH AVENUE, NEW YORK, NY 10010

Printed and bound in Italy

Contents

ARCHITECTURAL DESIGN PROFILE No 110

ASPECTS OF MINIMAL ARCHITECTURE

Maggie Toy Editorial 6
Clare Melhuish On Minimalism in Architecture 8
Pip Vice Minimalism and the Art of Visual Noise 14
Ricardo Legorreta The Inspirations, Traditions and Humour in his work 18
Solana, Southlake/Westlake, Texas 20
Conrad Hotel, Cancun, Mexico 21
Alberto Campo Baeza More with Less 22
Gaspar House, Zahora, Cadiz 24
Public School, Cadiz 26
Turégano House, Pozuelo, Madrid 28
Garcia Marcos House, Valdemoro, Madrid 30
Claudio Silvestrin Architecture of Lessness 32
Barker-Mill Apartment, London 36
Johan Menswear Shop, Graz, Austria 40
Pawson Williams Architects Contextual Minimalism 42
Jean Nouvel The Cartier Building, Paris 46
Richard Meier & Partners Canal + Headquarters, Paris 50
Royal Dutch Paper Mills Headquarters 54
Herzog & de Meuron Goetz Gallery, Munich 58
John Pawson Rothman Apartment, London 62
Richard Gluckman Architects Marlborough Gallery, Madrid 66
Gagosian Gallery, New York 68
Barto + Barto La Pérouse Hotel, Nantes, France 70
Van Berkel & Bos 50/10 Kv Distributing Sub-Station, Amersfoort, The Netherlands 74
Tony Fretton Photographer's Office, London 76
Tod Williams, Billie Tsien and Associates The New College, University of Virginia 78
Pierre d'Avoine Architects The White House, London 80
Donald Judd The Chinati Foundation, Marfa, Texas 82
Ushida • Findlay Patnership Truss Wall House, Machida, Tokyo 84
Katsuhiro Isobe Dislocation: Landscaping Ring Zones, Amsterdam 88
O'Herlihy + Warner O'Herlihy House, Malibu, California 90
Tadao Ando Vitra Seminar House, Germany 92

EDITORIAL
MAGGIE TOY

The evolution of the International Style in the early years of this century was heralded by manifestos which proclaimed the beauty of architecture without ornament. Many key architects of the time developed an obsession, with the 'clean' architectural space defined by function and devoid of applied decoration – clean, efficient and tranquil. The results were intended to provoke positive emotions and acted as a breath of fresh air in contrast to the styles which had previously reigned.

Eugéne Grasset was a supporter of that which he deemed an appropriate use of ornament. In 1907 he declared that 'ornament is referred to as stylisation, the outcome of a voluntary act which transforms the natural object'. Others were appalled at the very concept of improving upon the natural object. In his famous script of 1908, Adolf Loos declared that 'cultural evolution is equivalent to the removal of ornament from articles of daily use'. Le Corbusier was quick to confirm these cultural and social implications; quoting from Loos he affirmed that 'the more cultivated a people becomes, the more decoration disappears'. And so the continued inextricable link between social, cultural and philosophical values was firmly re-established. Ludwig Wittgenstein's treatises added the necessary academic weight to this passion for simplicity. In partnership with the architect – and former pupil of Loos – Paul Engelmann, Wittgenstein built his sister's house in Vienna which embodies his ideals of 'functionalism, perfectionism and elegance as a consequence of truthfulness in thinking and acting'.

The beauty of simple elegance which was then established is partly responsible for the development of the Minimal design strategy we see today. The motivation for these thinkers and others of the time was of a political nature, eradicating the bourgeoisie desire for extravagance within its homes and buildings and replacing this with a universally accessible utilitarian ethic.

The Modern Movement is a style of architecture which requires a certain discipline. By definition styles are not universally accepted and therefore should not be forced where not desired or applicable. In addition, the idealistic motivation became slightly perverted. The Czech Cubist architect Pavel Janak wrote that 'Modern architects . . . behaved very materialistically, wanting to base their creations on construction of materials, because of the expression of and the animation of materials which comprised a materialistically narrowed principle . . . the growth of architecture as a responsive, formative and spiritual creation corresponds with the silencing of the material and construction elements and their subordination to the artistic intention'. He sets out the argument for creating an architecture which does not succumb to the pressures of an economically based construction industry and which allows original principles to remain consistent.

This quest for one all-encompassing architectural style no longer controls architecture – we now live in a pluralist age – but the continuation of the intention and beliefs of an architecture without applied ornament, a Minimal architecture is clearly demonstrated within this issue. There is a clear perception of the freedom afforded to its inhabitants, to experience tranquillity and liberation from conventional distractions, through the medium of an uncluttered environment. At a time when some architects and urbanists are using chaos and complexity theories as a method for creation and explanation of architectural and urban environments, it is important to recognise the merits of the contrasting Minimal condition.

The sheer stunning beauty of the schemes created by the architects featured here indicates their dedication to the Minimalist ethos. It can be extremely expensive to achieve the craftsmanship necessary to attain perfect, finely detailed finishes. What exists is a determination and discipline which allows an organised minimal existence. This is widely used as an interior solution, but equally exquisite when adopted for the individual house, as in the case of Silvestrin, Pawson and Campo Baeza. Similar principles – although slightly diluted – are employed by architects, such as Meier and Nouvel, in the execution of their solutions to the demands of the larger, more complex projects. The motivation behind the work of Ricardo Legorreta is that of redefining a vernacular architecture of which Mexico can be proud.

Today's Minimal architecture encompasses that sense of place, and the style is not encumbered by any economic panacea philosophy. It has incorporated the good objectives of Modernism with the benefits of hindsight. If the maxim is true 'Freedom of the mind is created within the strictest routines', then the principles of a Minimalist architecture are an indication of true cerebral and practical liberation.

OPPOSITE: Tadao Ando, Forest of Tombs Museum, Kumamoto, Japan

CLARE MELHUISH
ON MINIMALISM IN ARCHITECTURE

If someone bothered to feed the facts into a computer – and maybe someone has – it would probably be possible to predict in exactly which of the years ahead skirts would be long, mid length or short, trousers narrow or flared, colours pastel or vivid, and cuts sharp or relaxed, allowing clothes to be put away in the wardrobe with a ticket indicating when they would next be in vogue. Such is the mechanism of fashion: an even turning of the wheel from one polarity to the other in rhythmic accordance with the time it takes for humans to tire of one thing and crave its opposite.

Fashion holds sway in architecture and design as well, although because each part of the cycle takes longer to come to maturity, the wheel turns more slowly, and its movement not perceived so clearly. So when, amidst a plethora of glossy magazine articles on the same subject, the 'minimal' approach was hailed as 'the style of the nineties' in Jonathan Glancey and Richard Bryant's book *The New Moderns*, it was not entirely surprising, after a decade of excess and conspicuous material consumption by the richer elements of society. As Glancey so aptly put it: 'some wealthy people are tiring of the visual clutter and sheer bulk of too many worldly possessions and discarding these in favour of more austere homes.' The magazines stopped showing the wild and wacky homes of rich eccentrics and fell over themselves to picture cool rectilinear interiors constructed out of natural materials, painted white, or at least in neutral hues, stripped of conventional detailing, bathed in natural light, and cleared of all superfluous furnishing to make way for a single Modern classic, or, alternatively, some piece of ethnic booty from, say, Tahiti, to emphasise the flight of the sophisticated from the consumerism of the developed world. Suddenly it was all very chic: recession chic.

Once society has tired of the austere look, as it moves out of recession in the inevitable economic cycle of boom and slump, it will no doubt revert back to some form of the voluptuous and overblown. Yet underneath the fashionable froth, beyond the reach of the glossy magazines, there is the steady undertow of a serious international architectural tradition of illustrious descent which has been flowing with renewed strength since well before the beginning of the 1990s – at least ten years before. The term 'minimalism' had had some currency in architectural debate for some time prior to 1990, in connection with the work of a number of architects emerging around the end of the 1970s, who had espoused a lean, pared-down approach to design. In December 1988 a special issue, entitled 'Minimal', of the Italian architectural magazine *Rassegna* was devoted to an analysis of the phenomenon; it only needed Charles Jencks to launch it officially in popular architectural culture as a distinct new movement in late-20th century architecture.

When Jencks published his book *The New Moderns* [1] almost simultaneously with Glancey and Bryant's volume of the same name, it seemed the moment might have come: a proof that something must be going on beyond what merely 'some wealthy people' were doing, which would be of significance to Jencks' exclusively architectural readership seeking an insight less into lifestyles than into new developments in the architectural debate.

Jencks had previously made use of the term minimalism in his book *Current Architecture*, in 1982, but only in a fairly casual, adjectival, rather than generic sense, with reference to the work of Koolhaas, Hejduk, Eisenman, Campi and Pessina.[2] Confusingly, he uses a capital 'M' on each occasion, but never actually defines what it means – Koolhaas is influenced by the Minimalism of Mies van der Rohe, Hejduk by the 'Minimalist image', and Eisenman by the Minimalism of Donald Judd while Campi and Pessina make use of a 'Minimalist' pediment. In fact it is the simpler, more linear work discussed in the chapter on 'Twenties Revivalism' which seems most closely related to the minimal 'new modernism' outlined by Glancey and Bryant. Surprisingly, this work is hardly mentioned in Jencks' own *New Moderns*, which is more concerned with a fragmented type of architecture – 'Neo Modernism'. Minimalism itself is only briefly defined, as an essentially bourgeois, Late-Modern movement. This definition was repeated a year later, in the new additions to the sixth edition of *The Language of Post-Modern Architecture* (1991). Minimalism was linked to Deconstruction, Avant-Gardism, and silence used to describe the work of architects Antoine Predock and Luis Barragan, but again left largely unexplained.

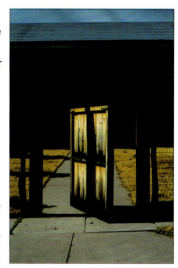

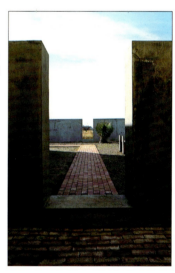

OPPOSITE: Alberto Campo Baeza, Public School, Cadiz; ABOVE AND BELOW: Donald Judd, The Chinati Foundation, Marfa, Texas

The architects who appear in the Twenties Revival category (which he traces back to the mid-1960s) of Jencks' flow diagram of architectural trends, as published in *New Moderns*, include Tadao Ando, Benson and Forsyth, Tod Williams, Kurokawa, Meier, Holl, Gwathmey Siegel, George Ranalli in the 1980s, and Colquhoun and Miller, Neave Brown, Botta, Lasdun, Hejduk, Aymonino and others in the 1970s bracket. This is a fairly broad range, both stylistically and chronologically, but there are overlaps with the contents of the Glancey/Bryant book, in which Holl, Gwathmey Siegel, Meier and Ando also appear. Jencks however does not include any British architects of the 1980s, while Glancey and Bryant are mainly concerned with precisely that generation of British architecture: Mather, Chipperfield, d'Avoine, Wild, Chassay, Munkenbeck and Marshall and Pawson and Silvestrin – who came to notice in the 1980s.

However, there remains a considerable degree of consensus between Glancey and Bryant's minimal 'new moderns', and Jencks' 'Twenties Revival' architects – although more limited correlation with his sketchy references to minimalism itself (Barragan is probably the only one of Jencks' minimalists who would fit into the Glancey/Bryant new-modern stable, except that his work uses bright colours). Furthermore, Glancey and Bryant specifically refer to Le Corbusier, Neutra, Frank Lloyd Wright and Chareau as influences on the new modern architects they discuss; while Jencks describes Mies van der Rohe himself as a progenitor of Minimalism. The connection with the architecture of the early Modern Movement is thus implicit in the current usage of the term 'minimalism', widely understood as being in some sense a revival of early Modernist aims and forms.

There is a certain amount of truth in this. The interest in openness and continuity of space, generating an essentially horizontal architecture, the reduction of detailing to the minimum, along with the rejection of traditional architectural forms and conventions, and the play of natural light on mainly white surfaces, are common to both generations of architecture, and give the work a certain similarity of appearance. But the key difference is in the concept of the 'minimal' itself.

Although not a term given any currency in connection with the Modern Movement at the time, it has since been used by Alan Colquhoun to describe its failings: 'one of the strongest criticisms of modernism was directed against the architectural version of minimalism, closely tied to the doctrine of functionalism.'[3] In Colquhoun's mind, the concepts of functionalism and minimalism are 'bound together'. But there is a world of difference between the early Modern pursuit of a mechanistic and industrial reinvention of architecture ('the house a machine for living in') – the functionalism, as an end in itself, which eventually generated such a backlash – and the interest of current, so-called 'minimalist' architects in fulfilment of the functional programme simply as a means to an end, being the corporeal, sensual experience of uncluttered space.

Hence the connection between current architectural 'minimalism' and the ideology of the Modern Movement has to be handled cautiously. The implications of the term as used in the architecture debate, which the Jencks and Glancey/Bryant books extended to a wider, more general audience, have also to be understood in relation to the art movement of the same name, represented by the work of artists such as Donald Judd.

It is notable that in all the serious magazine coverage of the architectural debate on 'minimalism' – *Rassegna*, December 1988, *Lotus* 73, 1992 and *El Croquis* 62-63, 1993 the architectural content is paralleled by substantial discussion of so-called Minimal art, acknowledging and highlighting the strong links between the two disciplines. Minimalism emerged in America in the 1960s, as a new movement which spread into painting from sculpture, led by figures such as Dan Flavin, Carl Andre, Robert Morris, Robert Smithson and Richard Serra as well as Donald Judd. It had been prefigured by the work of Ad Reinhardt, Barnett Newman and David Smith, developing as a new impetus to constructivism, and also called primary structure, or ABC art – in which there are strong overtones of the Bauhaus.

The minimalist sculptors and painters 'aspired to muteness and can be regarded as a further reductionist development in abstract art', according to Frances Spalding, although they never welcomed the name the critics gave them, with its negative overtones, just as most architects now will only reluctantly acknowledge it.[4] Their work paralleled that of the Pop Artists, in that it rejected the ideal of the work of art as either a vehicle for personal expression, or for any other sort of intellectual or metaphysical meaning over and above the 'meaning latent in different materials and in the processes of making' (Michael Craig-Martin, *The Art of Context*).[5] Their strategy, however, was the reverse of the Pop artists': whereas they sought to evade the process of 'interpretation' by choosing a content so obvious and banal that it became meaningless, the minimalists pursued the same aim by reducing all content as far as they could to nothing.

Hence the abstract materiality of the art became paramount – 'the simple, irreducible, irrefutable object', as EC Goosen put it, in an essay for the catalogue to the 1968 exhibition at the Tate, London, aptly entitled *Art of the Real*. The intention was to displace intellectual,

Pierre d'Avoine Architects, White House, London

cerebral perception and understanding of the work in favour of pure physical, corporeal and sensory experience, on the grounds that: 'Words restrict experiences and ideas as well as develop and organise them. We become slaves to the limitations imposed on us by our use of language, at the same time that we organise ourselves in essential ways because of it' (Allen Leepa, in *Experience: The Spectator*).[6]

The phenomenological nature, architectonic purity and relationship to site of the work of the minimalist artists has undoubtedly been extremely influential on the younger generation of contemporary architects throughout the Americas and Europe as they reassess architectural values in the aftermath of Venturi and Post-Modernism. In 1966, two years before the Tate's *Art of the Real* exhibition of American minimalist art, Venturi had published *Complexity and Contradiction in Architecture*, in which he condemned orthodox Modernism, as inculcated by Gropius, Mies van der Rohe and other representatives of the Bauhaus in America after 1937, for idealising 'the primitive and elementary at the expense of the diverse and the sophisticated', and 'puritanically advocat(ing) the separation and exclusion of elements, rather than the inclusion of various requirements and their juxtapositions.' Venturi called for a fresh understanding of architecture as a vehicle of communication, or a 'language', rich in the meaning and signification inherent in cultural and social history: precisely the opposite of what the Minimalist art movement stood for, at precisely the same moment.

In 1972 Venturi published *Learning from Las Vegas*, containing his theory of the 'decorated hut'. Although the reaction against his ideas had already set in, with the emergence in the same year of the New York Five (Eisenman, Graves, Hejduk, Meier and Gwathmey), calling for a return to the first principles of Modernism, the impact of *Las Vegas* was to be felt in architecture across the world for at least the next 10-15 years, achieving, perhaps, its most potent symbolic expression in the architecture of Disneyland, in Florida. The New York Five can arguably be seen as predecessors of contemporary Western 'minimalism', in their early reaction against the post-modernist manifesto for an architectural language based on historical precedent, and their pursuit of a rather self-conscious abstraction in which the austerity associated with the early Modern Movement was tempered by lyricism and a certain fulsome, almost figurative quality. Twenty years on, Richard Meier and Charles Gwathmey are still working in very much the same idiom on a large scale; while Graves has absconded to the camp of Post-Modernism itself, Hejduk has embraced a certain intellectual esotericism apart from building, and Eisenman has diverged away into Deconstructivism.

It is in the substitution of austere functionalism by what can be an almost too consciously composed, too perfectly crafted, poetry of materials in light and forms in space that the significant difference between early Modernism and the new architectural minimalism lies; and, likewise, the firm common ground between architectural minimalism and the minimalist art movement, reinforced by the flight of many architects from the dry, formal intellectualism of Deconstruction – from the need for 'interpretation' – which has succeeded the decorative excesses of Post-Modernism. Hence, although there is still a strong sense of the continuing, mythical 'unfinished project' of Modernism, and although the influence of Le Corbusier and Mies van der Rohe, especially, is still a powerful inspiration, although perhaps now equalled by that of Lloyd Wright and Kahn, and the later work of Corb, there is also a strong awareness of difference and new direction among the contemporary generation.

The minimalist idiom is not then simply a revival of early Modern ideals; and there is a further area of significant difference between the two, beyond, but interconnected with, the rejection of functionalism for materiality and sensual pleasure, which is the powerful influence exerted on the new generation of work by the awareness of different regional architectural traditions, in contradistinction to the universalism espoused by the Modern Movement. Of all of these it is probably the traditional architecture of Japan, and its modern-day interpretation by contemporary Japanese architects such as Tadao Ando, which has been the most profound inspiration to many architects in Europe and America. The effect of the simplicity, lightness and pure planar linearity of this architecture is summed up by Jun'ichiro Tanizaki in his influential essay on aesthetics: 'the beauty of a Japanese room depends on a variation of shadows, heavy shadows against light shadows - it has nothing else': a paradigm for a minimal architecture.[7]

The Japanese tradition seems to have been particularly influential on the work of British-based architects working in the minimalist idiom – perhaps because, geographically, the two countries share the constraints of limited space, and the condition of being surrounded by water, and, temperamentally, both races tend to reserve and, traditionally, an almost formal standard of courtesy. Of these architects, John Pawson, who believes the first use of the term 'minimalist' to describe a certain type of British architecture, was by an American critic in 1983 of the flat he had designed for himself, spent four years in Japan, where he had intended to enter a monastery, before beginning his architectural training at the AA. Here he met Tadao Ando, still at the

Richard Meier & Partners, Canal + Headquarters, Paris

beginning of his career, and forged a close friendship with the architect Shiro Kuramata, who was a strong influence.

Pawson's work during the 1980s consisted mainly of flats and houses in London for rich clients, many of whom were associated with the commercial art world. The work is almost obsessively concerned with the play of unadorned planes and volumes in light, the textures of materials, and the revealing of empty space. Between 1987 and 1989 he worked in partnership with fellow minimalist Claudio Silvestrin, who had established a reputation as a designer of commercial art galleries during a period when most gallerists were moving towards the ideal of the neutral space as the most appropriate setting for art. There is clearly an overlap between the two fields of work, in that many gallerists saw their homes as places for the display of art almost to the same degree as the gallery; but there was also an extension of the ideal beyond the work of art to the person. The human body, too, became an object in space, the architecture its setting. At one level, this represents a positive rediscovery of the body as the subject of architecture: a resurrection of architecture's human purpose after the tyranny of functionalism. But at another, Pawson and Silvestrin's work is of the sort that can seem almost too perfectly composed, too perfectly crafted, and thereby to negate the very physicality and earthiness of the human body. Both architects are aware of this problem. Pawson says, 'the danger is that the work becomes an artwork; then you lose the restraint.' It is the restraint which he regards as essential in creating 'calm spaces, a seamless effect', rather than falling into the trap of 'doing something clever' which he believes is a problem for so many architects – and even for the 'minimalist'.

Despite his experience in Japan, Pawson argues that there are other factors at play, coming from within the European tradition: the notion of casting away material positions for a life of contemplation is common to monastic traditions the world over, and nowhere, perhaps, more inspiringly expressed than in the architecture of the Cistercian monasteries, which he counts, along with the honest, industrial architecture of Halifax, the town of his birth, and the work of Mies van der Rohe, as possibly a greater influence than his experience in Japan.

Pawson and Silvestrin's work is perhaps the most extreme form of what is known as 'minimal' architecture in this country, but since the early 1980s there has been a considerable range of work perceived as belonging, broadly, in this area, largely to distinguish it, for the purposes of the critics, from either the architecture of structural and technological ingenuity and innovation represented by, say, Foster or Rogers, or the architecture of figuration represented in different forms by Farrell or the later work of Stirling.

According to Tony Fretton, the common quality of the so-called 'minimal' work is 'a reductivist quality . . . which is good', but he stresses that beyond the stylistic similarity is a whole range of very diverse ideas, and, unlike John Pawson, finds the term 'minimalism' 'not very useful.' Pierre d'Avoine also reiterates the essential quality of 'paring down' and 'reduction' in the work, but rejects the concept of minimalism as a style or an aesthetic. Both architects agree there is a common vocabulary of detailing across the whole range of the work, which Fretton describes as a rejection of traditional architectural vocabularies, and d'Avoine as 'a sort of mannerism, or inversion' and a reaction to the chunky, DIY-aesthetic detailing of the 1960s and 1970s.

Fretton's best-known work is the Lisson Gallery, designed for very much the same world as Silvestrin's galleries, but quite different in spirit, if not at a cursory viewing. Fretton's architecture is informed by a lively political agenda, and an awareness of its role in the world beyond its walls. The Lisson Gallery incorporates the rough edges of the real world, both within itself, and through the connections forged between the building and its immediate context: a scruffy street market in a still predominantly working-class area of the capital. Fretton is thus forcing the world of refinement and sophisticated taste into some form of engagement with the rough everyday life of the less privileged, and vice versa. This potential for conflict filters through the architecture itself, in total contrast to the calm perfection of Pawson or Silvestrin's work.

Fretton acknowledges the influence on his work of a type of neo-modernism based on the early Modern Movement, along with Louis Kahn's re-working of Modernism through the Japanese tradition. By contrast, d'Avoine, despite considerable experience of working in Japan, believes his work to be explicitly English in its genealogy, in the sense that it is part of a long tradition of leanness and linearity in English art and architecture. Nikolaus Pevsner, in his discussion of this subject, refers to 'the anti-corporeal flatness noticed throughout English architecture and the anti-corporeal intricacies of line noticed in some English architecture and in much later illumination', from Perpendicular architecture and psalter illustration, to Adam, Blake and Soane. He describes the linearity of English art – 'thin, wiry, sinewy . . . flaming or flowing' – as a 'negation of the swelling rotundity of the body' in favour of disembodiment. He also refers to 'a nausea of perfection' which led to the abandonment of the Early English for the Decorated style of architecture.[8]

Like Fretton, d'Avoine abjures the 'perfection' of Pawson or Silvestrin's approach, which he

John Pawson, RK RK shop, London

believes 'subjugates the user', but his work lacks the austerity and rough edges of Fretton's, expressing a potential for transformation rather than tension. Although he shares the predilection for a planar architecture of walls and uncluttered spaces, rather than structure, there is always a sense of latent movement and of the surprising in his work, and also a deep concern for the relationship of the architecture with its physical site. In the case of the White House, in London, an introverted suburban house is opened up in such a way as to transform not only its internal spaces, but also the street on which it is situated.

In view of the quantity of work produced in this country in the minimalist vein, it seems surprising that the British contribution has been almost completely overlooked in serious European coverage of the subject, overshadowed by the very strong Spanish, Italian, and, to a lesser extent, central European movements in this direction. Part of the reason may be that so much of the British work is still internal, while the opportunities to build in the round have been much greater abroad during this period. Part may be that the minimalist approach seems so alien to the Arts and Crafts movement with which Britain is so strongly associated abroad – although in fact the concern with materiality and craftsmanship is an area of common ground between the two – or the structural engineering tradition which is so admired, that the idea is too difficult to entertain.

On the other hand, the British have been deeply inspired by the work of Portuguese and Spanish 'minimalist' architects such as Edouardo Souto de Moura and Alvaro Siza of the Porto school, or Herzog and de Meuron and Diener and Diener of Switzerland – though less so by, say, the Italians Gino Valle or Francesco Venezia – all producing very different buildings, but, again, with the emphasis on 'the suppression of redundancy in artistic practice', as Vittorio Gregotti has put it.[9] The work is clearly related to that of the early Modern Movement, but the significant difference is always in the connection between the building and its site – whether urban or rural – and the craftsmanly, as opposed to industrial, quality of the construction. The mediterranean region has its own indigenous tradition of a simple geometric, strictly rational, whitewashed architecture integrated with the landscape, which José Luis Sert discussed in the 1930s as a basis for a humane contemporary architecture, and the spirit of this tradition seem to permeate the work of these latter-day mediterranean modernists.[10]

Beyond Europe, the most substantial amount of new architecture in the minimal vein is found in Japan, but the work produced by architects such as Ando, Shinohara, Maki or Isozaki is arguably a different thing from western 'minimalism', being so much a part of a centuries'-old indigenous architectural tradition rather than a specifically new development. In America, there seems to be surprisingly little current minimal work by the younger generation, though George Ranalli's interiors, and some of Steven Holl's, constructed out of simple geometric, white-painted volumes inserted into existing spaces could be included in the survey. It seems possible that the reason for this may be the fact that the origins of the Modern Movement in America were always imported, and that since then a reaction in favour of rediscovering a truly American, non-European architectural idiom has taken place, in which the more dynamic, expressive work of architects such as Frank Gehry has attracted most attention.

Ultimately the question with current minimalism is how long it will sustain its current appeal for younger architects. Undoubtedly its flowering has been closely associated with the escalation of world-wide economic recession and the steady growth of awareness of the need to conserve the world's resources if ecological collapse is to be avoided. In this context, minimalism, as an architecture of restraint and limited means, against over abundance and squander, has exercised a deep appeal. But as the cycle turns it seems not unlikely that reaction will set in, and the urge to make more dynamic, more exciting, more actively communicative architecture will return again. On the other hand, the qualities and ideals of minimal architecture may prove to be enduring; for as life itself becomes increasingly fragmented, intangible and uncertain, the innate human desire for the calm space, the comfort of solid materials and the contemplation of slow-moving nature, may become ever more powerful.

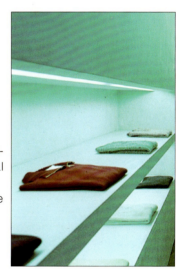

Claudio Silvestrin, Johan Menswear shop, Graz, Austria

Notes
1. Charles Jencks, *The New Moderns*, Academy Editions, London, 1990.
2. Reprinted and expanded as *Architecture Today*, Academy Editions, London, 1988 and 1993.
3. Alan Colquhoun, *Modernity and the Classical Tradition*, MIT Press, Cambridge, Mass, USA, 1989.
4. Frances Spalding, *British Art Since 1900*, Thames & Hudson, London, 1986.
5. *Minimalism: Collection Display*, Tate Gallery, Liverpool catalogue, March 1989-Feb 1990.
6. *Ibid*.
7. Jun'Ichiro Tanizaki, *In Praise of Shadows*, Leete's Island Books, 1977.
8. Nikolaus Pevsner, *The Englishness of English Art*, Penguin, London, 1956.
9. Vittorio Gregotti, 'Minimal', *Rassegna*, Dec 1988.
10. José Luis Sert, *Mediterranean Architecture*, Poligrafa, 1974.

PIP VICE
MINIMALISM AND THE ART OF VISUAL NOISE

Stravinsky, in *The Poetics of Music*, asserted that the better the artist, the more he limits himself to making his music out of as few as possible pieces, the more he abstracts it. Minimalism is essentially a reductionist architecture with a subdued palette of colours, a sophisticated level of finish within a highly controlled structure. It comprises leanness, shedding away, space, linearity, sophisticated simplicity and contemplation.

But is it still relevant today? Does Minimalism as a 'style' of the 90s exist? As Tony Fretton remarked, had this question been asked at least four to five years ago a very different answer might be given to the ones that now exist – namely that the strict format of Minimalism has remained while the issues have changed. Now architects are thinking in different terms. Indeed, this has also filtered to other media. A Sheffield-based graphics company, The Designers Republic, whose client list consists almost entirely of record companies, says how detail has almost become an addiction. Not so much 'less is more' as 'more is more'. Perhaps this is a turn around for the 90s in opposition to the currently expressed maxim that Minimalism is the style of the 90s. The 80s perhaps.

It is no coincidence that British architects are currently working abroad where they are able to secure more commissions than in Britain as in the cases of David Chipperfield, Pierre d'Avoine, Tom Heneghan and Kathryn Findlay who are all working/have worked in Japan. It would appear that places such as Japan and India are more receptive to the formulas of Minimalism, their ways of living, traditions and the weather all make Minimalist architecture ideally suited for hotter climes. It seems no coincidence that it is also 'flourishing' in Mexico with Ricardo Legorreta and in Australia with architects like Mitchell/Giurgola Thorp, Denton Corker Marshall and Bob Nation.

Minimalism can trace some of its many roots in diverse architectural movements such as de Stijl and Bauhaus, with de Stijl's reduction of individual variations to a minimum and Adolf Loos' white, chaste, austere, understated, anti bourgeois, anti eclectic buildings; later developed by Gropius and Le Corbusier. The New York Five (The Whites: Eisenman, Graves, Gwathmey, Hejduk and Meier) in their turn reveal a quest for the purism of Le Corbusier. And yet Minimalism is also a reaction to the bursting consumerism of the 80s which in the 90s has been translated as 'back to basics' with very different results. It can also be seen as a Westernised absorption of some of the tenets from Japan (like Japan we are a small island with more people than space). The Japanese genius for enlarging limited space is well known. While in Japan, particularly cities such as Tokyo/Osaka appear chaotic and haphazard with more time spent at work than in the home, the home is a place of tranquillity. It is a secular shrine where shoes are left outside and a very different lifestyle/philosophy is led to that of the West. So, Minimalism has taken a part of Japanese tranquillity and translated it for its own ends. With their low perspective (sitting on cushions/mats at low tables); paper covered lanterns; finely grained smooth wood; sliding doors; the use of natural materials (although highly worked) and subdued colours/shadows a feeling of space is achieved. While our perspective is turned into the home, the Japanese look out of theirs (again enhancing the feeling of space) onto the street or a purposefully abundant garden.

But what are the strengths of Minimalism? Although there have been adaptions there are certain elements that remain. Primarily it is the ease, calm and soothing nature of the architecture that ensures its survival. Tod Williams and Billie Tsien's design for the Go Silk showroom in New York is seen as a soft, tranquil haven. As the buyers 'dash in from chaotic Seventh Avenue or from other showrooms in the same building, you can almost see them sigh with relief' as they enter the building. As a work environment, simply, 'it's soothing'. Lines flow smoothly, spaces are as important as the placing of objects and even the smallest spaces are highly controlled. Fretton has remarked on the beautiful designed spaces in the changing rooms at Stanton Williams' Issey Miyake shop, London and Claudio Silvestrin's Gravity & Grace installation at the Hayward Gallery which he says is completely convincing in its form.

Much has been written on the metaphysical aspect of Minimalism; but it is also a sort of Puritanical theory where the less the distraction the less difficult it is to concentrate on God. And what is being contemplated in the Godless latter half of the 20th century? Claudio Silvestrin writes how through contemplation of the object, 'envisionment of the perfect' is attained.

Why, however is Minimalism not a puritanical

OPPOSITE: Claudio Silvestrin, Gravity & Grace installation, Hayward Gallery, London

architecture? It is leanness, it is starkness, it is purity, simplicity and denial; however it is not looking out to God but is personal. Simplicity of form does not necessarily imply austerity of lifestyle but it does give very little reflection of self. A room laid bare, with as few objects as (unessentially) possible in subdued hues, evokes the lifestyle of the owner as much as Minimalism evokes a certain type of lifestyle itself. Western ways of living have inherited a tradition of amassing objects to adorn and decorate the home, different to the eastern conception. One cannot imagine normal family life continuing in its regular haphazardness way in a Minimalist home, even if everything can be hidden away in spacious cupboards; for children are essentially reflections of self and possessions, both of which are somehow denied or reflected by Minimalism. It seems significant that the kitchen (as well as restaurants, cafes, bars, shops and particularly art galleries) are more suited to the lean style in the west than in the home. (Could it be no coincidence that Philippe's surname is Star(c)k?)

Just how simple is the Minimalist lifestyle? In order to *choose* to live simply requires careful and meticulous design and concentration and adherence in order to carry it through. There is a difference between those who have a few carefully selected possessions by choice and those who have few possessions by lack of choice, lack of time and lack of wealth. Ironically those with wealth seek fewer objects while those without covet more. As Tom Wolfe wryly noted in *From Bauhaus to Our House*, the working classes nearly always disliked the white abstractions made in their name and preferred to live in houses which were more polychromatic and exuberant.

What happens when we approach Minimalism in other media, cinema, music, theatre, literature, fashion and food? The film director Peter Greenaway could be called the enemy of Minimalism; he is very much of the more-is-luxuriant-is-sexual-is-significant-is-velvet-school. Film is by necessity a visual medium and doesn't translate well into the Minimalist medium because it is, in the broadest, most basic sense, about visual, cathartic entertainment; *ie*, a distraction.

Bare, empty spaces in films are only used for atmospheric setting, character portrayal, period setting or script. For example Alain Delon in *Le Samourai* is a solitary professional killer whose room consists only of a chair, a bed, a bird in a cage and packets of *Gauloises* reflecting his hitman way of life. His dialogue is almost as minimal as is Gabriel Byrne's in David Drury's efficient thriller, *Defence of the Realm*, which is suitable for the role of an investigative tabloid journalist. Or *Mishima,* the highly stylised biography of the writer Yukio Mishima which calls, in parts, for some stylised filming (appropriately with music by Philip Glass). It would not be enough to have the empty, spartan spaces etc throughout an entire film. Minimalism has difficulties translating into film; as a non static medium itself film cannot easily show the contemplation of Minimalism as by its very nature it moves too rapidly, in seconds.

It is interesting that the ultimate Minimalist film (in one sense) was created by a director dying of Aids with visual impairment which showed only a blank, bright, light, blue screen. Derek Jarman's *Blue* essentially became a film that not only showed the pain he was suffering but could only relay his ideas as a film director nearing the end of his life, with 'nothing'. Ironic that the visual medium in this case became, essentially, aural; ie, that the visual screen could not adapt itself to portraying the visual lessness and thus moved to a different medium: sound. Even in Japan, directors such as Yasujiro Ozu and Akiro Kurosawa give us a visual feast of colour (in the latter's case) and detail.

But that Minimalism should have to be accessible in different media does not necessarily point to its success or failure as a style/lifestyle. Purity of form can be achieved within the visual medium as artists such as Donald Judd, Josef Arbers, Rothko and Barnett Newman showed by reducing art to its barest essentials. (His son, Flavin Judd stated that, 'Donald hated the word Minimalism', and Tony Fretton, speaking for most architects states, 'Along with everyone else I am sure, I disclaim all knowledge of Minimalism!' In sculpture we have the precedents in the classical Cycladic folded-arm figurines with their sloping wedge heads which are objects of supreme purity and simplicity; these works were translated into the modern arena by Brancusi, Picasso and Moore.

It would appear quite apt that the idea of *nouvelle cuisine* should appear in times of massive conspicuous consumption. Bite size, beautifully served dishes (ironically Westernising the Japanese tradition of cooking and serving) all contribute to a sense of purity and simplicity. While thin is in, on the one hand we have the lifestyle of all work and hard play.

Less is more is certainly the maxim for Western high-life living in terms of the figure (especially, if not exclusively, for women) where thinness denotes restraint, unindulgence, control and above all, beauty; not to mention the 'guilt' associated with First World excess amid Second/Third World poverty. (In the fashion world we now have the rise of the waiflike super model which is less than minimal.) Fat is to be despised as a lack of discipline, *ie* conspicuous consumption. Minimalism in one sense is an adopted poverty, possibly an assuaging of guilt of excessive wealth in an increasingly polarised society.

John Pawson's Canelle cake shop, London seems entirely appropriate for the idea of denial and lack of self indulgence. 'A mask facade is

John Pawson, Cannelle Cake Shop, London

punctured by a clear glass cube, just large enough for the display of a *single* (my italics) cake set at its centre'. Any clutter is hidden behind the marble and steel counters placed behind a low wall. It is the anorexic's dream, as opposed to the usual nightmare glut of sticky desserts, almond croissants and tarts groaning behind the glass counters. This sort of selling in a round about way subverts the very idea of selling in the conventional sense that what distinguishes us in the West is that we have choice and lots of it.

Again we have the self-denial, the breaking away from excess. When inundated with visual, sound, air and light pollution the only answer is to retreat into silence.

'Less is more' in shops (clothes as well as food) is not (as is the case in Russia and some Eastern Bloc Countries) there by necessity, but by design. What you buy does not come in abundance but comes in pared down choice, good quality, natural ways. Perhaps this is the consumers'/consumerists' misunderstood translation of Minimalism; or perhaps it is merely another facet of its development. Certainly we are now very used to seeing the slightly more up-market clothes shops on the High Streets that have taken some of the facets of Minimalism and used them to, on occasion, great success. Wooden floors, pale colours, discreet lighting, natural fibres, metal chairs are more or less visible in clothing stores, The Gap, Jigsaw and Whistles and abroad such as Country Road in Australia. Further north from the south-east there is the German owned chain of shops Netto where goods are left in their packaging boxes and choice and packaging has been reduced: by necessity.

Restaurants and cafes have also taken parts of Minimalism (the use of natural materials, metal and wooden furniture, subdued colours, light) and converted them to their own ends. Munkenbeck and Marshall's recent project for a restaurant, Orsino, London uses the natural fibres, subdued hues etched with slightly more blushing colour and the spartan bathrooms (where more than one customer has had difficulty in finding how to turn on the taps/flush the toilet etc).

It would appear that art galleries are in one sense best adapted to clear, plain spaces. Fretton's Lisson Grove art gallery is white and empty, it is an abstraction of colour and abstraction of form – in Donald Judd's words architectural renovation is an 'act of purification'.

How is Minimalism to develop in the future; indeed, has it survived up until now or has it been translated to become another form where we now have such labels as Contextual Minimalism, Organic Minimalism, low-tech Minimalism etc?

As Angeleno Josh Schweitzer has said of his own work, 'I think my work is Minimal in that it deals simply in form, color (*sic*) and light without special attention to intricate or elaborate details. .

.' His project house, The Monument, composed of simple geometric forms is intended to function as a series of rooms to complement the landscape (its location is the Joshua Tree National Monument park, Los Angeles). The house is constructed of simple materials, the colours echo those of the desert, 'it is simplicity of form, not the perfection or purification of it . . . that is the goal of the architecture. . .'

Site is an important aspect of Minimal architecture and, as in Schweitzer's work, has also contributed to the work of Mitchell/Giurgola Thorp in its project for a holiday retreat at Whale Beach, one of Sydney's northern coastal luxurious refuges. MGT has remained true to its simple, geometrical approach to architecture, 'a modern classicism that combines an almost spartan delineation of space with elegant finishes and materials.' The house blending in and using its environment contributes easily to the Minimalist use of space and has echoes in Alvar Aalto. Evans and Shalev's St Ives Art Gallery in Cornwall also contains the idea of easy harmony between the building and its surrounding landscape. Australia's Denton Corker Marshall's house near the sea on Philip Island, Australia, is intended to be, 'another dune in the landscape. . . there is no particular play of light and shade, no interaction of volumetric form, no colour . . . Its role is to abstract itself until it is a non-event . . .'

Trevor Horne has mentioned how nowadays we are tending to use things more as they are found and not designing to the *n*th degree. The self-referential aspect of Minimalism is perhaps becoming more outwardly accessible with another dimension added to it. As Horne mentioned, 'It takes a lot of tenacity to design Minimal architecture. . .' Rather like Capability Brown in the 18th century who designed with the utmost attention to detail and last blade of grass or ha-ha, to make gardens for the gentry appear casual and 'natural', so Minimalism requires this restraint and tenacity to obtain simple, clear forms.

Perhaps then, Minimalism needs to an extent to be 'humanised', to be, tautologically, pared down; it needs the misunderstandings and slight changes in order to develop as more than just a lifestyle reduced to a coterie of knowledgeable and astute conformists.

However, architecture has to be inhabited, and as Charles Moore wrote, 'One could certainly make the case that many famous buildings, especially in our own century, don't have any quality of making you feel in repose in the middle, of them, don't even have the capacity to let you connect with them, even to the point of finding the front door so you can get in. . .' Going through the front door is what it's all about.

Richard Gluckman Architects, Marlborough Gallery, Madrid

RICARDO LEGORRETA
THE INSPIRATIONS, TRADITIONS AND HUMOUR IN HIS WORK

Working in Mexico, Ricardo Legorreta, throughout twenty five years of practice, has not only established himself as a worldwide leading architect but has also retained his Mexican vernacular. He has cited the influences in his past as that of his father, José Villagran and in particular the work of fellow countryman Luis Barragan whose architectural details have frequently been quoted in works from Legorreta through to Claudio Silvestrin.

Legorreta admits that each person has his or her own way of doing things, especially when this involves a creative activity. For him the most important matter in designing is to establish a design philosophy. Each building needs and should have its own appropriate principle that directs the design.

He has written that when he receives a commission, his life starts spinning around it. 'I think it, I see it and I live it. I spend several weeks without drawing or sketching; during this time I think all day about the project, while dressing, eating, listening to music and especially while looking at books and visiting places of inspiration that have some relation to the problem. . .

Little by little the philosophy of the building starts to take shape in my mind and suddenly I have the feeling that it is ready. Then I draw. When that moment comes I feel a very special excitement, I feel like taking the pencil and I start drawing lines, squares, circles, and shapes, and the piece of paper becomes alive, my imagination flies, and the shapes are created, architecture appears . . . this is the moment of inspiration!. . . '

For Legorreta the intellectual approach to architecture, that is, an approach that needs explanation, does not necessarily help to shape a good building; the intellectual approach can restrict the imagination and by extension destroys the emotions that are so important in creating architecture. It is reason versus emotion. It is a process that can be compared with love. As he has written, 'intellectual love does not forgive, emotional love has deep roots. Spontaneity in designing leaves a trace of the designer's feelings and releases the observer's own imagination to dream with architecture. Usually, I dream of colour, walls, mystery, intimacy and other qualities that matter in particular to me as a person, and as a Mexican.'

Legorreta follows the usual stages of

FROM ABOVE: Solana, Southlake/Westlake, Texas, exterior and interior; Hotel Camino Real, Mexico

development in his planning and design, overseeing every detail, from the masterplan through to the essential minutiae such as light fixtures and door knobs. This is the scope of his architecture. 'I love to go to the construction site, too. Before that, the building is just drawings. At the construction site architecture takes place. My reward as an architect is when I go alone to the construction site and experience the spaces, light, colour – the architecture that is emerging.'

Legorreta retains a certain humour in his works. It is not the sophisticated humour accessible only to a few *cognoscenti* but is available for all who view his buildings for the first or tenth times. The Hotel Camino Real, one of Legorreta's works of the late 60s, reveals that the playfulness inherent in his work has always been a constant thread which does not detract from the highly serious and important aspects that also exist. The Hotel does not possess the lack of character evident in many contemporary hotels; instead it is lively and adheres to the Mexican vernacular in using brightly coloured sun-dried brick. There are many interior courtyards and the hallways are filled with works of art. Space is exploited fully in the corridors, the staircases and the lobbies, and the playful element is constant.

An architect friend of Legorreta's having visited the hotel wrote that he had had, 'The pleasure of getting lost,' while staying there. Legorreta is never predictable but is always vigorous and full of life. His understanding of people manifests itself in his work and the basic enjoyment that people obtain from seeking. He has always maintained that architects must serve the people for whom they design and not pander to their own intellectual ideas or theories.

This does not imply that Legorreta is disillusioned with his profession. On the contrary, the very fact that a person can marvel at a curve in a building, or a wall or a beam is what divides architects from non-architects. It is at this time, Legorreta writes, 'when I realise I have the most beautiful profession in the world. It allows me to think spiritually. I believe something a friend said to me: "Give thanks because in your profession you have the great opportunity of participating in the completion of God's creation."'

FROM ABOVE: Metropolitan Cathedral of Managua, Nicaragua, views; Renault Factory, Gomez Palacio, Mexico

SOLANA
Southlake/Westlake, Texas

For a 1,900-acre property of rolling hills and working with the clients' desire to develop a unique concept, a team of four architectural firms, Mitchell Giurgola, Barton Mayers, Peter Walker and Legorreta Arquitectos, developed a very simple scheme that took advantage of the highway that crossed the property. In a parkway that crossed the property, an underpass was designed so it formed part of the architectural concept.

The main objective was to recover the original prairie and to create compounds that would establish their unity by the interplay of the scale of limiting walls, height, colour and fenestration proportions of each building; permitting an overall unity and offering each architect his freedom of designs. Vertical elements were created as directional and entrance symbols. Walls, textures and colours were carefully used to humanise the almost unlimited scale of the Texas landscape to more intimate human spaces.

The village centre comprises two office buildings for rent, a shopping and offices compound, a 200 room hotel and a health and sports club. The IBM phase I-A building comprises offices, dining room and computer centre.

The design concept is a series of buildings and courtyards, incorporating the landscape, the highway and the underpass, to create individual and intimate spaces.

LEFT: Site plan of Solana village centre

CONRAD HOTEL
Cancun, Mexico

The climate, the water and the sand of Cancun, the special form of the terrain and its position between the sea and the lagoon, all make Conrad Cancun an exceptional place.

The architectural project adapts to these conditions. It is based on simple, elongated forms which permit guests to enjoy the sea or the lagoon – depending on the time of day, whilst taking advantage of the spectacular views and the presence of water.

Making full use of the breeze, allows life in the majority of the public areas to continue in a natural manner, without the necessity of air conditioning.

ALBERTO CAMPO BAEZA
MORE WITH LESS
Essentiality

I propose an ESSENTIAL Architecture of IDEA, LIGHT and SPACE

IDEA

An Architecture that is born of an IDEA

Without an IDEA, Architecture would be pointless, only empty form

An IDEA which is capable of: serving (function), responding to a place (context), resolving itself geometrically (composition), materialising itself physically (construction)

Architecture is always a built IDEA. The History of Architecture is the History of built IDEAS. Forms change, they crumble, but the IDEAS remain, they are eternal

LIGHT

An Architecture is brought into existence by LIGHT

Without LIGHT Architecture is nothing

LIGHT is an essential material in the construction of Architecture

LIGHT is that which creates a relation, a tension between man and Architectural space

SPACE

An Architecture is translated into an ESSENTIAL SPACE

SPACE is shaped by FORM through the minimal, indispensable number of elements capable of translating the IDEA with precision

A SPACE is capable of touching people

More with Less

This Architecture, born of an IDEA, shaped by ESSENTIAL spaces and tensed by LIGHT, allows people to find in it the BEAUTY that only Architecture is capable of offering them. That BEAUTY which is always the final stop on this long journey towards Liberty, which is CREATION

With these notes on IDEA, LIGHT and ESSENTIALITY, I offer here some of my work in which I have attempted to translate this simple principle of 'MORE WITH LESS'

PRECISIONS I

About ESSENTIALITY

ESSENTIAL Architecture (Not Essentialist) is NOT MINIMALISM

ESSENTIALITY	is NOT	EssentialISM
	is NOT an	ISM
	is NOT a	MinimalISM
	is	ESSENTIALITY
	is	Precision
	is something more than only a question of Form	
	is a	BUILT IDEA
	is	POETIC
	is	MORE WITH LESS

ESSENTIAL ARCHITECTURE is NOT cold and cruel
is NOT perfectionist and untouchable
is NOT imposing and overwhelming
is NOT only to be photographed

    is CLEAN and SIMPLE
    is NATURAL and OPEN
    is FREE and LIBERATING
    is FOR LIVING

I would like my ARCHITECTURE to be:
    as PRECISE as Bernini's, as luminous
    as NATURAL as Barragan's, architecture for the man
    as DESHABILLÉ as Le Corbusier's, as strong and powerful

not for the purpose of becoming famous
but making man happy

not only for this time
but forever

not to be photographed
but to be lived

PRECISIONS II

About the perfect perfectionist work

(Praise of IMPERFECTION)

I think, like Heidegger, that architectural spaces tensed up by the LIGHT are to be inhabited by the man

I think, like Barragan, that creation is of cleaner and more free spaces, it s not the creation of hard, cold and untouchable ones. Architectural spaces are to be inhabited (they are not freezers)

I think, like Le Corbusier, that the creation of spaces for man calls for a level of imperfection (*deshabillé*) which underlines the power of architecture

Architectural spaces should house man not expel him. In this way the Parthenon, the Hagia Sofia or the Pantheon have all housed man in History (they are admirably corroded)

And even more than perfect and unpolluted houses, I prefer:

The imperfect Villa Savoie by Le Corbusier
The decorticated houses by Barragan
The huddled Villa Malaparte by Libera
and
Melnikov's own defective house in Moscow
Utzon's own corroded house in Palma

And I discover in them that the History of Architecture is the History of IDEAS, of BUILT IDEAS, of magnificent imperfect works with magnificent LIGHT which provokes a magnificent life, Emotion in man and intelligent Beauty!

GASPAR HOUSE
Zahora, Cadiz

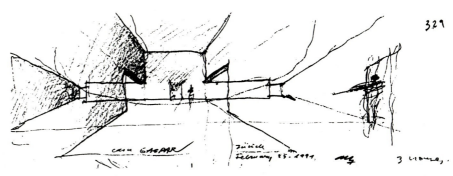

Hortus Conclusus – (Closed Grove)
On the day that the artist came back from the sea drenched in light, wearing only salt and crowned with foam, and arriving at the orange grove he decided to establish his resting place there.

With his back to the sun and facing his own long shadow, he pointed with his outstretched arms the four cardinal points which defined a square. He made the floor out of stone and walled in with four, high, white walls. In the wall which faced the sunset, he opened a door, and after crossing its threshold, he was enclosed into this serene walled enclosure.

Once inside he divided the square into three equal parts, raising two with walls higher than the surrounding walls. He put a ceiling on them creating a patio in front and another one behind. In it he opened another door to enter into a higher and darker space.

Once inside he pierced and shaped the white wall, chiselling shadows with light. Raising the other walls he established prodigious relations.

He planted four green lemon trees, two in the patio in front, and the other two in the patio behind. And there, in the back, ending the axis of all the doors, he dug a grave from the earth from where the water came to sing, waking up the lemon trees in white lemon blossoms which flooded the air with the scent of Paradise.

And the artist thought that this space of the *present absence* full of light and silence and beauty, was preferable to the medley outside in which our society was racking.

And seeing that that which he had made was good, he rested there to live happily ever after.

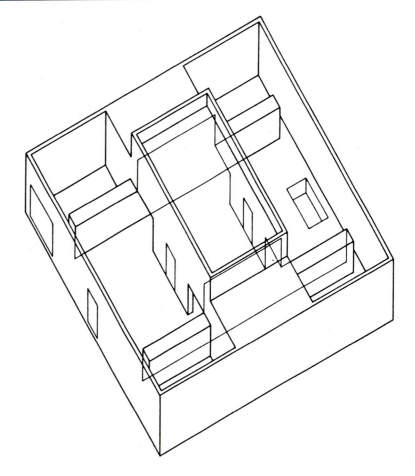

ABOVE AND BELOW: *Conceptual perspective sketch; axonometric*

PUBLIC SCHOOL
Cadiz

Looking at the Sea
Cadiz, the oldest city in the Occident, has always had its eyes open to the sea. Lots of times, 'a sea of times', its buildings have been raised over themselves. The city raised its look-out towers – today the archetypal image of Cadiz is to be able to look out towards the sea.

The school faces the west horizon of the ocean where the sun is hidden by a different colour with every sunset. At the same sea side, continuing the powerful and lime painted walls of the marine cemetery of Cadiz, and between the sea and our site, is a road. There is always a constant, intense light streaming in.

The building's most public spaces – the main hall, the library and the cafeteria – open out to the landscape and to the light which comes through these high and big holes. The main hall creates a tension with the diagonal light which connects the deep vertical hole to the sea with a precise perforation opened in the ceiling on the opposite wall. Through the main staircase the platform is reached which materialises a free plane. This plane floats on the infinite Atlantic Ocean which is framed by this deep hole.

The library and the cafeteria incorporate this exceptional panorama through another hole with its double-order, which is perforated in its highest and deepest point so that it can be pierced by the sunbeams. The projected solid light emerges from the shadows of the big white wall, putting the space in vibration. In the heart of the building there is a white patio, an abyss of brightness, which works like an articulating mechanism of corridors and classrooms. Four erect palm trees underline its square geometry.

The strong salty scent and the constant murmur of the waves emphasise the palpable sensations of light and shadow, brightness and darkness, serenity and freshness. Once more, there is the attempt to get maximum beauty with minimum elements. MORE WITH LESS.

Conceptual sketch

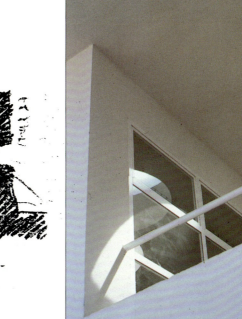

TURÉGANO HOUSE
Pozuelo, Madrid

The fable of the happy architect and the white and cubical hut

Once upon a time, in an old country, there was a young architect who passionately loved architecture and who, the poor fool, was an artist who thought of and built houses. He was a thinker who built. He was a builder who thought. And thinking and building, dreaming and making his dreams come true, he was immensely happy.

In this same country there were other architects who believed they had exclusive possession of intellectuality, who were convinced of being the only ones in possession of the truth.

And they despised the artist. They said 'He builds! He builds and so he gets dirty!' And they called the artist contaminated, uncultured, out of tune with his times, impure.

In this same country, there were other architects who believed they had exclusive possession of professionality and who were also convinced of being the only ones in possession of the truth.

And they despised the artist. They said 'He thinks. He's got his head in the clouds!' And they called the artist a radical, they accused him of being hard, of not having his feet on the earth, of being rigorous, a purist.

And between these two furious, stormy oceans, our architect, serene, became strong on his island-self where, happily, he thought and built.

He thought and in his thoughts, conceived handsome works that could and must become reality. He built and there rose up graceful fabrics that expressed those ideas with wonderful clarity.

'I plan as if I were carrying it out. All I think of is do-able, and what I do is in agreement with everything intelligible', he repeated with the Eupalinos of his beloved Valéry.

And he took pleasure in considering that the beauty of his work arose from that built-up thought. 'Without ideas', he said, 'there cannot be any good architecture; architecture is more than just forms.'

'Without building', he explained, 'there cannot be a true architecture. Architecture is something more than just an Idea'.

And so thinking and building, dreaming and making these dreams real he was, is tremendously happy.

One day, what a happy day! our ever-young architect, the artist, dreamt of living within an idea: in a white and cubical hut. Because he had always thought that instead of searching for Paradise and therein the Hut, it was a question of building the Hut and with it Paradise! Once more the myth of the primitive Hut! 'To succeed in being able to build an ideal in order to live within it', reasoned the artist, 'must be the height of happiness for rational man'. To live within an ideal! To live within a dream come true!

On the following day, and how long was that day that lasted almost more than a year! our artist, with the help of other madmen who understood him, set to work and built the idea!

And how his heart beat when those walls were going up that proclaimed that that reality was possible!

And how his spirit trembled when the *light*, caught up, decided to remain for ever among those walls!

And how all his being vibrated with emotion when *beauty* penetrated radiant into that space, never to leave it! The artist thought he would die of happiness.

And on the third day, this day still lasts, he rested. And he saw that what he had done was good. And he lived in that white and luminous house forever happy.

And the birds came to rest on it.

And the trees surrounding it offered their shade and their most enticing fruits.

And the breeze caressed the house as evening came.

And although the artist wished to take refuge in silence, the Light and Beauty and Architecture unceasingly proclaimed to the four winds that there something had happened.

Will somebody, sometime, somewhere succeed in hearing the song of these voices?

Conceptual sketch

GARCIA MARCOS HOUSE
Valdemoro, Madrid

Une boîte à miracles – (A box of miracles)
Can a mysterious white box – through the work and grace of architecture – transform itself into a light and large open house?

This conventional single family house is situated in the suburbs of Valdemoro. It is a white prism divided transversally into three parts of 2:3:2 proportions. The central part empties out in its total double height. The ceiling is perforated near the interior wall, producing the vertical entrance of light. The exterior wall is perforated in its lowest part, keeping the same horizontal plane on the exterior, thus making evident the continuity with the horizontal light brought in there. The diagonal light resulting from the conjugation of these two operations places this space under tension.

Fundamentally speaking, this project is conceived as an architecture of rooms, two on each side, articulated over the central space. The serving elements of the stairs and washrooms are situated on both sides of the main axis achieving an effective centring of the circulations. The swimming pool continues the horizontal plan and offers multiple suggestions and inspiration.

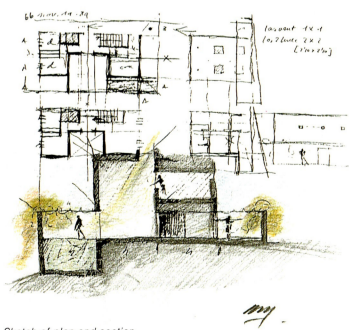

Sketch of plan and section

CLAUDIO SILVESTRIN
ARCHITECTURE OF LESSNESS

In his short story *First Love* Samuel Beckett speaks: 'She said I should have fetched my things. I explained I had no things . . . I surveyed the room with horror. Such density of furniture defeats imagination.'

Our man-made environment is an explosion of objects, millions of objects. We no longer transform natural things into artefacts that serve the whole cycle of Nature; we no longer revere nature as Nature: by imitation or representation of nature or by abstract artifice, we actually want to worship man as the subject.

Creativity, until not long ago pertaining to the space of divinities, has been posited in the space of the world-market. Today man pretends to create the world: he designs. In designing he intellectually 'naturalises' the market products, thus undermining the likelihood of questioning them. The object-design renders the equipment with apparent usefulness: to the piece of equipment the 'designer' adds an aesthetic value that adheres to it. The unity of art-science is therefore interpreted as handsome technology. The object-design seduces, it naturalises its usefulness: it must be used. The world-market gratifies the powerless individual who, blinded by the mythical happiness of the object, will never question such modern myth, will never question the structure of the world-market itself. Consequently, there arise no obstacles to the increased accumulation of clutter on our planet in the production of ever more 'uselessness'. Sick of this self-asserting decadence, I perceive configurations free from the illusions of a functioning technology: free from all presumed necessities, assumed utilities, the so-called commodities, the fabricated superfluous figures of our mundane vision. I see the horizon as a stable, calm, free, austere, clear, unimpeded line. Thus the passion to select, abstract, reduce and get rid of; to dispossess.

Reduction to simplicity is not nihilism. Nihilism is departure from simplicity: it occludes the clear vision of Being and, consequently, loses ground and meaning. In most classical art (and pre-classical works) the tendency is to reduce to the essence, to simplify, to abandon any superfluity. Thus the signs resembling the gods were certainly not considered superfluous. Their task was to reduce the phenomenon, the first appearance to its essence; to its symbol of its inexplicable existence. Cistercian architecture is the

FROM ABOVE: Claudio Silvestrin and John Pawson, Neundorf villa, Mallorca (x2); Claudio Silvestrin, Maison B, Provence

most clear example of beauty within austerity.

The tendency to simplify has manifested itself very clearly in the predominant art movements of the early part of this century: in it there is so much to learn. Most twentieth century artists, from Cézanne to the contemporary Fontana, Andre, de Maria, Judd and Serra, by de-constructing conventional codes and simplification to elementary forms, by freeing themselves from redundancies and representations, have been able to render the thing-itself. The black painted square of Malévich is nothing but a black painted square figure on white canvas. The black square on canvas is devoid of references or metaphors: the square is not painted as symbolic form, but as a primary form itself which does not intend even to represent itself.

It presents itself, it shows itself as revealing nothing but itself. Malévich wrote of his black square: 'I was grabbed by . . . a timidity bordering on fear when it came to leaving the world of will and idea . . . the reality in which I had believed. But the blissful sense of liberating non-objectivity drew me forth into the "desert". Where nothing is real except feeling . . . and so feeling became the substance of my life.' Kandinsky says: 'The bare wall is the ideal wall, the wall on which there is nothing, against which nothing is leaned, on which no picture is hung, on which there are no objects to see. It is self standing, it is in itself and for itself, it asserts itself . . . perfectly smooth, plumb, proportioned, mute, sublime. . .'

'Getting rid of' aims at seeing anew, a seeing that frees itself from any form of conquest, from any form of intellect, even daring to do without judgmental language: it pronounces clarity of Being at first sight; a seeing without the desire to possess. Quoting Maurice Merleau-Ponty: 'We must learn how to master that which pulls us towards things so that things are not the victims of our will to objectify because we end up being the victims.' Dispossessiveness and lessness are the words to act upon. Dispossessing of space is the first act. I think of space as mass of air; as breathing, as depth, as possibility for movement, as visual clarity.

Space is today seen as something to conquer. Politicians, technocrats and property developers interpret space as economical quantum, thus negating any possibility of free space. To them the cluttering of our planet does not suffice; now

Claudio Silvestrin, Maison B, Provence

they have started assaulting the cosmic space. Can space, as it is manifested in technological design, be said to be space?

According to Heidegger's research, the definition of the word space is 'to make-and-leave space; to make room for.' The making of space brings the openness essential for the settling and dwelling of humans. Making space prepares the site for habitation. This making room for and preservation of the space as space means placing, arranging and ordering in accord. This according, this taking of measurements, lets the open be. Openness – free space – gives presence to the appearance of things and humans. Measured placing gives to things the possibility of belonging to a site and, from this, the possibility of a relationship between them. The site opens up a free space whilst gathering the things together in their reciprocal identification with the open space.

Destroying clutter is seeing the 'thickness' of space, the depth of the world: not an object for manipulation, not a locus for clutter, nor something to conquer. Taking possession of space is precisely what is not wanted. The architectural work must open up space and preserve it. Unoccupied space is not useless or wasted or lacking. The emptiness in a jar, in a corner, in a lawn of a cloister is not nothing. On the contrary: the space in a wine glass is what makes the vitreous body a glass. Construction is not only producing; it is not only setting up and erecting: this is what technological building design is. The essence of construction lies neither in piling up layers of building materials nor in ordering them according to a plan, but solely in the opening up: when we set up a new space another 'atmosphere' opens up precisely through what is set up. Thus the architectural work is positing that construct: that is, it founds, erects and opens up a new seeing. This new seeing strives to be the envisionment of the perfect.

Walls make spaces irrespective of man. Man's self-assertive will wills the cluttering of such space. But the mute force which projects from a free wall 'is' space. Man, then, cleverly reduces such force by making walls mere supports for his objects, his possessions. In the principle of the cloister, walls make a perfect (enclosed) space: when we enter it we feel – space. The perfect configuration of few figures acts as spur to the imagination; it helps in perceiving the mass of air inhabiting the room that we call space. Each figure is enhanced by space and the few earthly materials reveal all their splendour. The earth is rendered by the purity of the materials' surrounding properties – surface, colour, thickness and weight – and not by figurative nature-imitation ornaments. With the minimum number of objects, of materials, of figures, of lines, of colours, of signs, the invisibility of space almost vanishes:

FROM ABOVE: Claudio Silvestrin and John Pawson, Neuendorf villa, Mallorca; Claudio Silvestrin, Barker-Mill apartment, London, interiors

space is, at least intuitively, visible. With this minimum we let space be present, space is no longer objectified, conquered. It is, rather, preserved as free space. It is held and grasped as 'thing' and no longer as object. It is this ontological sense of space that has to be understood. With this minimum we render our horizon with few and simple figures. With a visual and clear order of lines in equilibrium and in symmetry one feels at peace. The ideal configuration of elegant simplicity renders a feeling of serenity, of tranquillity; any form of struggle ceases, the cogito gives up doubting. When in a work there are geometric forms independent from metaphysical, theological or anthropological representation, they assert themselves, thus avoiding the speculative claims associated with personal authorship. When a form is not referential, when it is not delivering our nostalgic mnemonic images; in other words, when it is not negated by one's own self-assertive will, the geometric form appears ambiguous, indeterminable, a non-entity, suggesting a multitude of readings, a possibility for other possibilities, a possibility for a new sensibility. The ideal configuration frees one's vision from the fashionable objects which resemble finitude, thus the feeling of durable calm. The body of the ideal figures being of those earthly materials which 'are' solidity, immobility, peacefulness, renders a configuration like that of Raphael's portraits in which flesh is rendered to resemble plaster, clay, stone. Thus the feeling of durability, endurance; a vision of a world of figures immobilised in stillness: time is arrested, thought is suspended; figures in their silent presence, without a future or a past – in fatality. This is a vision of a place impregnated with grand calm, awesome.

The envisionment of the perfect demands a close understanding of the life elements and of the site materials; this is by far a superior criterion to that of novelty. The manipulation of materials, crafted with consistency towards perfection, transforms the material. The stone, dematerialised, loses its hardness. The wall, invisibly suspended, wins over gravity. The sun, piercing through deep and tiny openings, loses its overly glaring heat and is enhanced to its magnificence. The ideal manipulation transforms the site and yet the site is not disintegrated.

Architectonic poetry commences with dispossessiveness and lessness in our relationship with the things that surround us, with the site we stand on, with the earthly elements of the site, as well as with the architecture of the sky by which the site is enveloped. Hence the construction of a new scene with those materials and configurations that bring the site closer to us, that let the earth be earth, that make the sky nearer, the sun's splendour more intense, the night closer to night, the horizon open, the sound silenced, the space visible.

FROM ABOVE: Claudio Silvestrin, Gravity & Grace installation, Hayward Gallery, London (x2); White Cube Gallery, London; Victoria Miro Gallery, Florence

BARKER-MILL APARTMENT
London

The architect and the artists Adam and Carolyn Barker-Mill first met on the south bank of the river Arno in Florence at the opening of the Victoria Miro gallery, a space designed by Silvestrin for contemporary art amidst the Renaissance splendour of Florence. Maybe then it was no coincidence that in the summer of 1991, the Barker-Mills acquired a 2,500 square-foot apartment overlooking the south bank of the Thames between Albert and Battersea bridges, in the glass building constructed by Sir Norman Foster in the late 1980s, which offered panoramic views of the city. Silvestrin received a note which read: 'We have been discussing the idea of redesigning the interior of our flat at Riverside One, and we were wondering if you would like to create a Silvestrin masterpiece.' So Silvestrin started setting up a peaceful space despite the restrictions of being unable to intervene on the existing low ceilings and perimeter windows.

The first step was to open up the north-south axis, flanked on one side by a long stretch of floating solid white wall through which the cityscape projects run uninterrupted from one end of the flat to the other across the very large slabs of Tuscany pietra serena stone, which echo the calm grey winding of the Thames. A floor-to-ceiling curved satin glass screen separates the doorless kitchen and bedroom areas from the 'public' living room and study areas. As it separates it also reveals and unites the figures on either side casting silhouettes against its surface.

To the west, further screens act both as barrier to and enhancer of the outside light. Solid and stretched interior wall expanses carry Adam Barker-Mill's light sculptures, which have been incorporated into the wall's thickness.

The geometrical forms of the apartment's furniture are all one-off designs by Silvestrin, as are all fixtures and fittings from the flush lighting discs and elegant wood tap fittings to the stone kitchen island, bathroom basins and pear wood tables and benches.

Numerous sophisticated details veil the technology, with a configuration of silence and abstraction; all the functions being concealed behind the glass screens, floor-to-ceiling cupboard doors and walls. Everywhere, the materials are rigorously natural and their qualities come alive due to the monolithic pure forms through which they are presented.

JOHAN MENSWEAR SHOP
Graz, Austria

Johan, in the heart of Graz's traditional shopping quarter in Austria, is a new men's fashion shop. The premises are on the ground floor of a sober 16th century building and consist of two long narrow spaces with vaulted ceilings. These two spaces were originally rather pokey and gloomy but have been transformed into a streamlined futuristic interior.

Ceilings, walls, shelving, display tables and units are rendered in grey greenish pigmented plaster; the floor is covered with an almost matching smoothed concrete. This shadow coloured lining of the interior creates a peaceful background against which the clothes stand out like statues. The original facade proposed by the architect – a striking minimal curved satin glass wall stretching the whole width of the building – was rejected by the city planners.

The two sections of the shop comprise the main display area on one side, where the space's perspective is emphasised by the long stepped wooden display counter, which stretches down towards the back of the shop where a Fontanese stone bench runs from wall to wall in front of a screen of backlit satin glass and encourages one to sit, linger and look. The other section is visually separate and contains the menhir-like changing cabins, also rendered in the same pigmented plaster. These three playful structures shield the body but allow the head to pop out over the top. They are illuminated by natural light entering through a horizontal cut carved through the ceiling to the floor above. The lighting complements this serene space with its continuous fluorescent tubing hidden behind the perimeter walls. At the entrance to the shop, a monolithic display counter, made entirely of satin glass, juts through the clear glass facade and radiates light from within at night.

The clutter of cash registers and credit card paraphernalia is discreetly out of sight, leaving the space clear and free for the clothes and the bodies which inhabit them.

PAWSON WILLIAMS ARCHITECTS
CONTEXTUAL MINIMALISM

The architectural philosophy which has been developed by Terry and myself over the past five years has occurred by an interchange with the design process which we follow. Therefore, the technique of design that results in our architecture is not causal in the sense that there is always *a priori* a destined goal within any given project, predetermining the design response, which is then attained as though the designer were on rails. It is more a philosophy which defines hierarchical boundaries, a series of limits of possibility and exploration which develop from the specific nature of the project, its function, its site, its history, boundaries to which one may adhere or by careful consideration, transgress.

We consider ourselves Contextual Minimalists. This statement needs careful definition and amplification. The discussion, however, must be prefaced by expressing unequivocally, the deep belief which we hold, in the validity of abstract modernist architecture, to be developed continually in new directions, to give appropriate architectural expression to our thoughts.

Paradoxically, the collaboration which began at Kingston School of Architecture, developed later at Terry Farrell's office in the 1980s. The principal lesson learned from Farrell was a great concern with public space, and with the scale and texture of buildings. If our work bares little overt resemblance to Farrell's then that fact may be explained in terms of our osmotic absorption of his ideas. It may be seen as a parallel influence to our great belief in the validity of abstract compositional techniques and the search for the sensual qualities offered by a reductivist architecture, the principal aspiration in our design process.

So, if we consider ourselves Contextual Minimalists, the statement suggests that there is an implicit fusion of two different thought processes contained within the one idea, one responding to a set of pre-existing circumstances and the other looking by reductive means to synthesise an abstract representation of an aesthetic into its simplest possible expression.

To expand, making architecture is about making choices, which once made, exclude other choices. The choices one makes establishes a kind of testament and in this changing industrial age that testament must respond to new ideas and examine the possibilities offered between a building's architecture and its surroundings.

The use of pure modernist architecture as an approach to create, or add to, a city is in a sense a contradiction since, almost by definition, modernism eschewed the traditional notion of the city, and is essentially anti-urbanistic in conventional terms. It was defined as such by the early modernist planners, who argued that the traditional notion of the city must be sidelined in the search for a radical series of forms. The early modernists conceived architecture and the city as a radical abstract vision.

Yet if some architects work in a corrupted version of styles of past eras, or fail to address the future in their work, surely this ultimately represents a regressive series of cultural values and shows a society in intellectual decline. Paradoxically, it is the creative power that is made available by modern design, and the immense logistics of the construction industry, that has allowed us to radically alter our cities in a short time frame and on an immense scale, pursuing an essentially anti-urban architecture.

It may be fortuitous that it is not possible to revert cultural memory in the manner of a computer, which can simply be instructed to forget everything it has just learned, and start again from some prior point in time. But the modern movement was to exclude 'old', the 'traditional' to follow a new path with an architecture leading not only to a new means of formal expression but for a new more socially aware, open culture.

To illustrate the point directly, one might consider Trellick Tower in west London by Erno Goldfinger. It is a clear expression of the living city, a sensuous abstract grid, a sophisticated mix of maisonette and flat, where the enclosed horizontal circulation decks connect to the campanile-like vertical circulation tower, separated from the main slab but connected umbilically to it. The building stands above ground to be judged as a complex abstract matrix, a rhythmic composition. Yet the indigenous architecture of the district comprises two or three storey 19th century houses, which ultimately prevent a value judgement of the composition in purely sculptural terms as object, the terms on which it is most possible to support the building. It is impossible to escape the restraints of either context or of cultural memory in architecture.

The thought processes and radical abstract creativity of the composers of the early 20th century, may be seen as parallel to that of their contemporaries in art, sculpture and architecture. They shared a belief that theoretical abstraction in its own right would somehow, in denying the human condition, provide a new level of cultural achievement, a new expression to which mankind could then aspire, unshackled by the hierarchies of past cultural structures.

The composer Arnold Schoenberg, (1874-1951) sought through abstract synthesis of musical structure, a cleansing of the grand classical romantic tradition of the 19th century. His use of the abstract 12 tone series relied upon a serial development of the theme ensuring that no pitch was repeated until all 11 remaining in the sequence had been heard. This causal numeric abstraction of the music, Schoenberg believed, would provide modernism with the grand linguistic musical statement needed to ensure classical music's continuum through to the 21st century.

The influence of pure abstraction in music was to impact upon equivalent movements in other disciplines within the arts. In architecture, perhaps the most celebrated example is to be seen in the work carried out by the Greek composer Xenakis, in the studio of Le Corbusier. This collaboration around a singular aspiration of abstraction as art, occurred on several post-war buildings, most particularly the monastery of Sainte-Marie de La Tourette, where whole facades were developed and organised on a mathematical musical principle giving the proportions, rhythms and harmonies to architecture.
In the work of the minimalist Estonian composer Arvo Pärt, (born 1935), it is possible to see the modernist musical tradition developed in a new direction, more particularly how sensual minimalism can be clearly expressed in conjunction with the depth provided by a prior musical culture, and how this may be understood as a parallel explanation of our particular attitude to architectural composition. It is most easily understood by a brief study of the composer and his work of homage, *Cantus in Memory of Benjamin Britten*, composed in 1977.

In the 1950s Pärt, like many of the pre- and post-war modernist composers, was working with Schoenberg's 12 note series as a structural technique, and prime ordering methodology. His musical development, however, led him to follow a particular direction, to undertake a type of

Pawson Williams Architects, Primates Gallery, Natural History Museum, London

relearning. His experiences and search for his own music matured during the years that led to his immigration to the West in the early 1980s. During this time, he endured long periods of near silence, a tonal cleansing in the search for the music that he really wished to write. Silence in music is in a sense analogous to space in architecture. It is all pervading, the natural state of things until an event disrupts it. The tonal colour and restrained structure of the *Cantus* owes much to this process of self-deprivation experienced by Pärt and from years devoted to an in depth study of early liturgical musical traditions of Eastern Orthodox Church.

If the structural possibilities within music are personified in Pärt's work how can the parallel be examined in our own architectural terms? This might best be considered, prior to a detailed examination of our own architecture, to consider a summary of architectural legacy most aligned with our thoughts since it is from those sources that a vocabulary of influence or lexicon of ideas emerges.

Abstract Architecture: If there is a particular work that summarises most of our abstract predilections it is the Casa delle Armi, Rome 1933-35 by the Italian Rationalist Luigi Moretti. Moretti's work seems aimed at a reductivism, an isolated pavilion against a wooded backdrop standing free on its plinth as a pure monument. Whilst not attempting to suggest any historical link to Moretti, the potential for exploration with plastic form and space, and the ability to encompass both development and change, is evident both in the work of Meier and Ando, within a very restricted palette, and the late Sir James Stirling, in a broader formal vocabulary at his Braun factory.

The City and the Reading of Urban Space: The Nolli plan of Rome establishes very clearly the relationship between the formal set piece and the background grain of the city. Whilst these opposites are not symbiotic, clearly the power of the set piece is enhanced by the background grain. But is often the set piece which is the intellectual and cultural reserve of the epoch which created it. The Place des Vosges, in the Marais district of Paris, completed in 1612, is a perfectly proportioned plan geometry, couched in a romantic hierarchy and the prevailing political system.

The City and the Reading of Skyline: New York, Sydney, Florence, San Giminiano or Edinburgh are cities whose spirit is encapsulated or expressed within a skyline. The common thread is the desire to push structures into vertical space to colonise another zone within the city. It is possible to read the meaning of the principal forms in relation to the particular governing hierarchy at the time of development, whether the principal motivation be commercial, political or religious.

Circulation, Route and Promenade: The relationship between movement, space and architec-

Pawson Williams Architects, Centre Régional de la Musique et de la Voix, (CRMV), Argenteuil, Paris

ture produces a rich lexicon of extremes. Circulation as ordering device is most powerfully stated in the staircase ramp in the Belvedere at the Vatican. At the major scale, it may be considered as a negative cut of space within the city grain, or the reverse condition, a positive object in space, the bridge. The city which began by a gradual move to enclose space with buildings, in the extreme, totally subordinates it.

Engineering and Building Culture: The potential for engineering response to inform the expression of buildings is well documented, witness the contribution to architecture of Freyssinet, Nervi, Rice, Arup, and recently, Calatrava. The contribution each has made to the practice of architecture through their own single-minded inventiveness, and the utter clarity in their thinking is where we find the greatest empathy, which may be regarded as the unifying condition.

We view as fundamental the ability to understand the issues that pertain to any specific circumstance, in order that a meaningful intervention can be proposed by the design process. The initial search at the outset of this process is to establish the contextual key to the project, the frame of reference within which to work. Our initial design moves, therefore, seek to define the boundaries of possibility and are a reaction to a contextual understanding – Reactive design possibilities.

Our work utilises the contrast between old and new, solid and void. Simple statements but with a developed hierarchy which in the end lends a complexity and richness. The search for clarity is paralleled by a search for richness and sensuality for a quality of history firmly rooting a project both in its time and location.

The possibilities offered by abstraction are theoretically limitless, since it should always be possible to abstract continually any idea. What interests us is the harmony and sensuality which are to be found in the process of reduction of abstract composition to its simplest material form, allowing space and proportion, solid and void, light and shadow to dominate. The potential, as in Pärt's late music, is for a reductivist aesthetic combining tradition, abstraction and sensuality.

In short, Contextual Minimalism.

Whether this conception, can provide an aesthetic prolongation of the modernist tradition becomes a matter of test over time. Our search in terms of the development of our own architecture considers the sensual qualities of architecture, of space, harmony proportion, and light, of surprise, or of calm, of promenade, of ascent of view. What is certain is that the intervention of modernist architecture and its social vision *en bloc* into the city, imposed a new aesthetic. We have argued that it is impossible to revert cultural memory and so in finality, the legacy of modern architecture must be embraced to search for a future tradition.

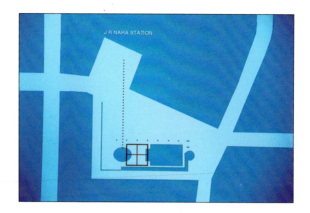

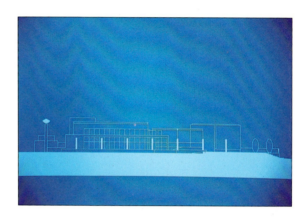

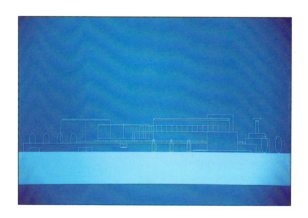

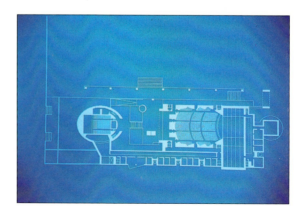

Pawson Williams Architects, Nara Convention Hall, Japan, showing site plan and entrance level plan

JEAN NOUVEL
THE CARTIER BUILDING
Paris

The first negotiations between Le GAN (the owners of the site) and Cartier began in 1991 to talk of a construction project for a building at 261 Boulevard Raspail. Its inauguration was held three years later.

The task was to create a special space and at the same time integrate art into the very heart of the business, through a versatile play of transparency, reflection and refraction with fine steel netting and glass. Large sliding bays disappear in the summer and the hall, now a rhythmical set of tall columns, becomes an extension of the park. The longitudinal facades reach beyond the main structure, while blurring its boundaries. The trees, as if gliding behind them, acquire an ambiguous presence.

The thin staircases are silhouetted in the light against the side walls. The glass panes extend beyond the terrace by a few metres. The west and south walls filter the light with their rolling blinds. Along the east facade, glide 'climber' type elevators, simple transparent volumes, without any apparent controls or cables. To the south, two metal *grilles* sink into the ground leading cars to the underground garage parking.

This is an architecture about lightness, glass and fine steel gridwork. An architecture whose rules consist in blurring the tangible limit, rendering superfluous the reading of solid volumes in a poetry of haze and evanescence and making clear its position on the notion of transparency and its alleged idle neutrality.

The luminous building fits gracefully into the natural environment of the park and generously opens itself to the city. It is a symbol of the future and perpetuity, and illustrates the willingness of the jeweller to merge with the extremely creative tradition of the great age of the Left Bank.

RICHARD MEIER & PARTNERS
CANAL + HEADQUARTERS
Paris

The new headquarters and production facilities for Canal +, on the left bank of the Seine just west of the Pont Mirabeau, are divided into a western wing for administration, facing the Seine, and a wide, eastern wing mainly for audiovisual production.

The general organisation derives from the overall context and some fairly severe site restrictions. The thin, tapering plan of the administration wing is a result of the northeast and northwest boundaries of the L-shaped site, which define two adjacent sides of a square park occupying the best part of the block.

Conceptually, Canal + depends on a series of delicately tessellated membranes. Of primary importance is the combination of clear, translucent and opaque white glass which make up the curtain wall on the river facade, in conjunction with the projecting, lightweight aluminium *brise soleil* along its entire length. A similar curtain wall is on the southern facade of the audiovisual wing facing the park.

All offices in the western wing face the river, and the building is backed by a metal-panelled spine facing the public park behind. Three large, four-storey television studios determine the basic shape and mass of the eastern wing, which is partially sunken to comply with the zoning envelope. Between the wings is a three-storey, sky-lit glass entry hall providing access to the studio floors.

The architects hoped that the aerodynamic thrust of the office wing wall opening to the river and the broad, contrasting mass of the studios would bring new life and a sense of civic destiny to this somewhat moribund wasted quarter of the city.

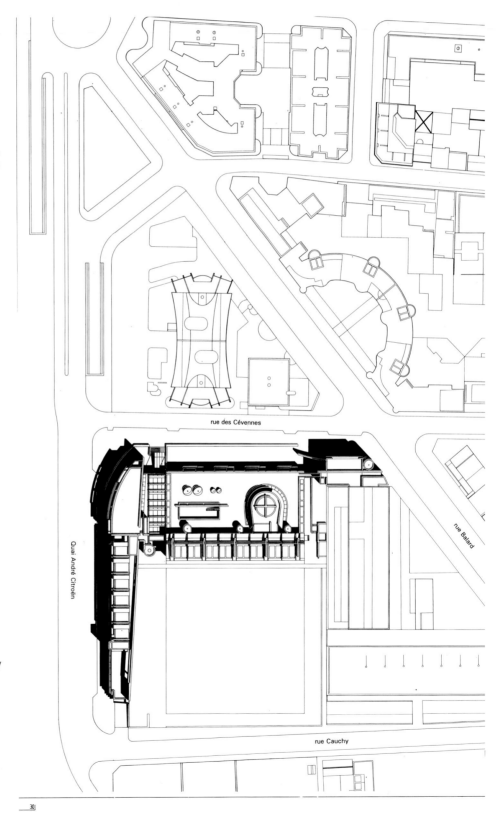

Site plan

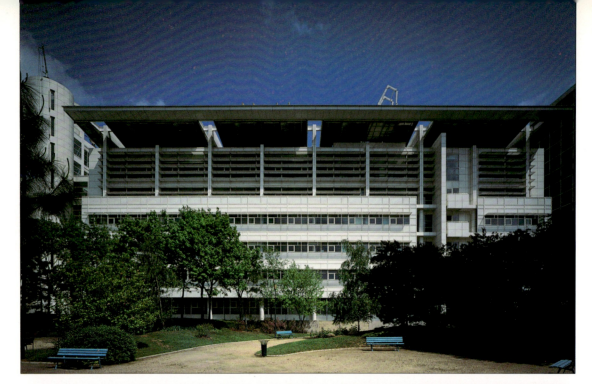

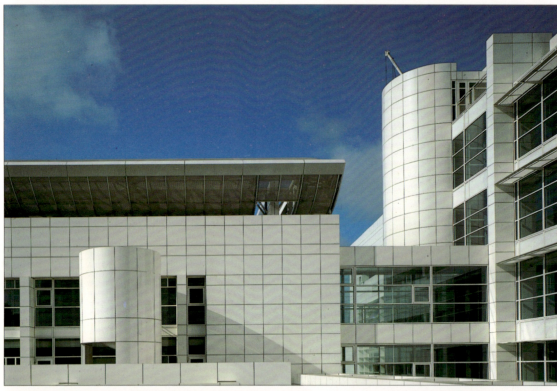

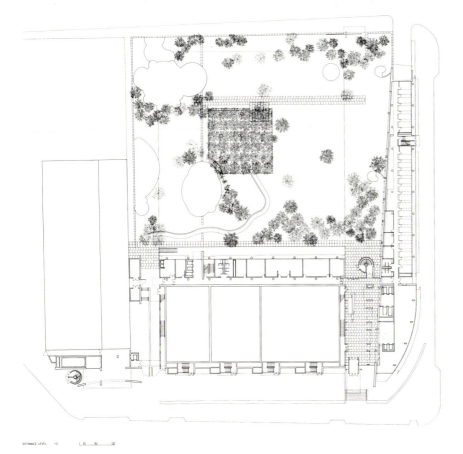

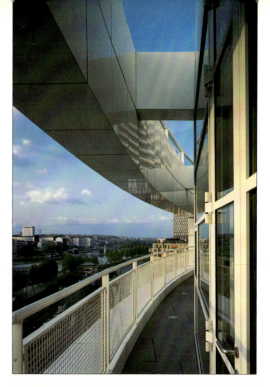

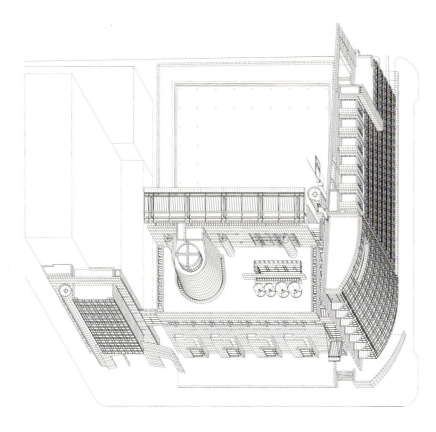

Entrance level plan; axonometric

ROYAL DUTCH PAPER MILLS HEADQUARTERS
Hilversum, The Netherlands

These headquarters, for a prominent international paper company, are designed for a pre-existing clearing in a densely wooded area. They consist of two linked structures: a four-storey cubic reception building and a two-storey office slab elevated above the greensward on piloti.

The reception building has dining facilities on the lower two floors, with the staff offices in the double-height ground floor volume and three private offices on a mezzanine looking down into it. The largest private dining suite opens to the south-west and has an outdoor terrace. There are guest offices and meeting rooms on the second floor, and a 60-seat lecture hall and conference room at the top.

The building is organised volumetrically around two intersecting service slots, with the elevator/mechanical core in one running north-east to south-west, and the intermediate waiting/service zone on the opposite axis. This area is flanked by a four-storey-high stone-faced wall that parallels an enclosed bridge on the first and second floors, which connects the reception areas of the two buildings.

The office slab has two principal entrances: one at the north-eastern end with a stairway, echoing a similar feature in the reception building, and another at midpoint with an elevator/stairway core for the executive offices in the south-western half of the slab. Both the executive and the staff offices are situated off a top-lit, double-height, double-loaded corridor with continuous access on one side and bridges to offices, in pairs, on the other. The office slab is based on syncopated counterpoint between the main structural bay, which is evident in the forms of flying beams and a secondary support system carrying the monitor lights above.

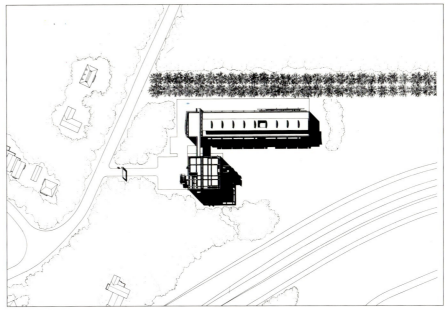

Site plan

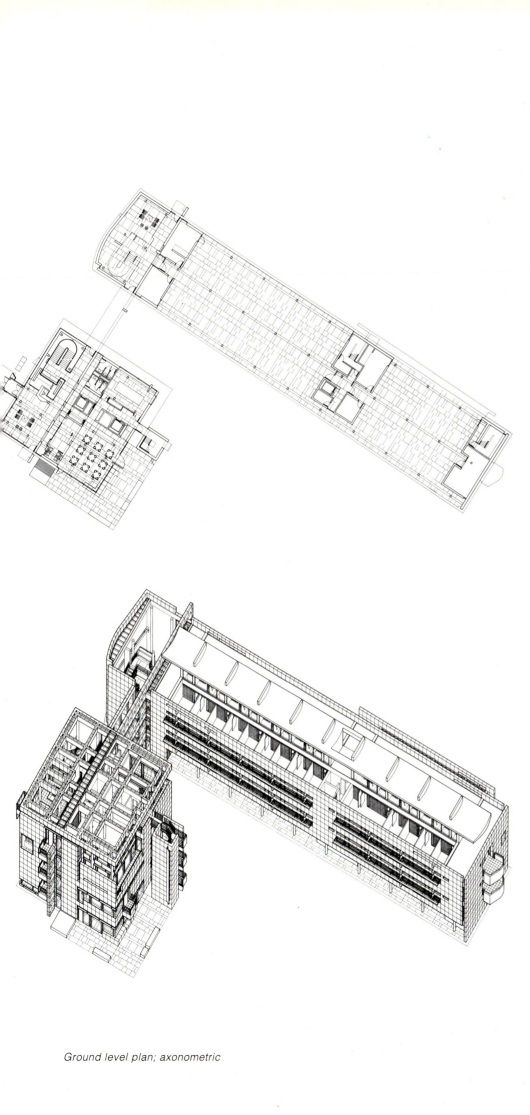

Ground level plan; axonometric

HERZOG & DE MEURON
GOETZ GALLERY
Munich

This gallery is a freestanding volume which is situated within a park-like garden of birches and conifers and between a street and a house from the 1960s. Thus, the building can be used both as a public and purely private gallery; a role that is to be settled in the future. The architectural conception of the building corresponds to the character of the works that the collector has brought together over the past thirty years, embracing art from the 1960s to that of today, namely Nauman, Ryman, Twombly, Kounellis, Federle, Ruckriem and others.

A timber configuration rests on a reinforced-concrete base of the same dimension which is half buried, so that only its upper glazed perimeter is visible from the outside. A similar matt glass strip surrounds the timber volume at the uppermost section, admitting diffuse glare-free daylight from a height of four metres into the exhibition spaces. The walls within the exhibition spaces are between 4.0 and 5.5 metres high.

Two reinforced-concrete tubes are set laterally between the lower and upper galleries. The larger of the two serves as the office and reception. Depending on the daylight conditions and the point of view of the observer, the gallery appears either as a closed, flush volume consisting of related materials (birch plywood, matt glass, untreated aluminium) or as a wooden box which rests on two trowels in the garden.

JOHN PAWSON
ROTHMAN APARTMENT
London

A single central element of deep cupboards running east to west between the exterior walls organises the public and private sides of the flat but still allows it to be viewed as a whole.

Natural light then becomes the main protagonist transforming the space during the day.

The kitchen is screened but not cut off from the sitting and eating areas. Bed, bath and study rooms can be closed off by sliding doors concealed in the walls and cupboards.

Walls of translucent acid-etched glass screen the washing area but allow light to travel both ways. Slabs of marble for the kitchen worktop, bathroom floor, basin trough and solid bathtub were hewn from a single block from Carrara. Japanese oak is used for the floor and the living room bench.

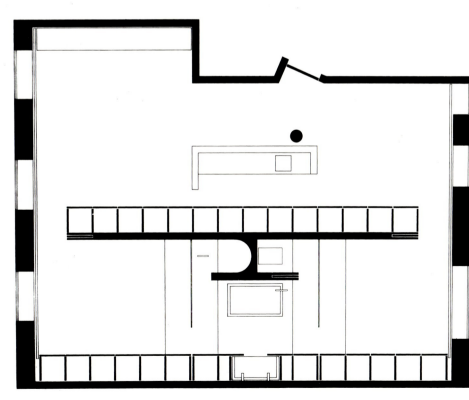

Site plan

RICHARD GLUCKMAN ARCHITECTS
MARLBOROUGH GALLERY
Madrid

The renovation involved transforming an existing ground floor space, sandwiched between the apartment block above and the parking garage below, into a commercial gallery. The existing glass block ceiling provided a unique opportunity to work with natural light. The scale and character of the exhibition spaces were defined by manipulating ceiling height and introducing new areas of glass block skylights.

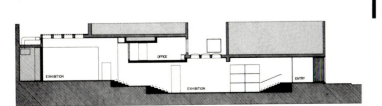

LEFT: Site plan; longitudinal section

GAGOSIAN GALLERY
New York

The Gagosian Gallery in SoHo is a large one room exhibition gallery, appropriate for the installation of contemporary art work. All that remains of the existing garage building is the brick facade. The floor and roof structure were replaced to maximise ceiling height and increase the floor's loading capacity, and a more efficient pier and wall structure were used to permit additional interior width.

Exposed beams, which correspond to the existing foundation structure, are revealed in the rationally placed skylight openings. Skylights provide a diffuse light throughout. Fixed point industrial halogen light fixtures are ceiling mounted around the periphery of the skylight openings.

The new concrete floor was burnished to provide a hard, dense finish, reminiscent of the building's industrial history. Control joints in the sidewalk and entry area correspond to the bays of the new garage door. In the exhibition space they are cut in large bays – in balance with the scale of the room and the works exhibited.

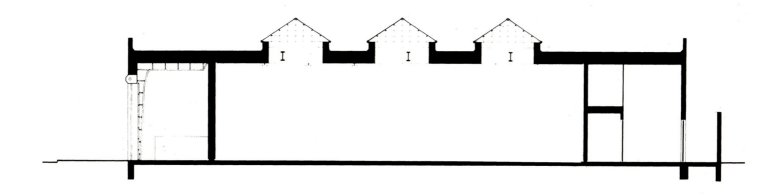

Sectional plan

BARTO + BARTO
LA PÉROUSE HOTEL
Nantes, France

In the heart of Nantes is the three-star Hotel La Pérouse. The architects had to integrate a building, controlled by the heritage sector, with the 20th century. In creating the building it was felt important to reject popular solutions, pastiches and currently fashionable designs – such as double skins, transparencies and mirror facades – in favour of rekindling past values which are all carried within us and which take the form of weighty, comforting and reassuring buildings.

But how could such values be created using modern construction methods? The answer to this was researched in detail. First of all classic references were investigated as were the period buildings of Nantes to ensure that the architecture would never appear alien, particularly not to Nantes itself. Strong references had to be drawn up initially so that the rest would take care of itself. This building was built specifically for Nantes and so it had to be embedded with local character and heavy and compact like other hotels which are unique to Nantes. It had to adopt the traditional style of roofs, buildings ending in blocks and identify its location: thus inserted into its urban reality.

In this project everything was executed to accord with the above ideas. The architects avoided returning to the codes written in the local city buildings. The horizontality of the buildings was underlined through the amplification and elongation of piercements within it.

Strength was created through vigorous treatment of wall angles and the roof. Strongly implanted in the earth, the building is endowed with presence. Ambiguity lies in the fact that it both rises up into the sky and plunges downward. Compactness is reinforced by using the same material for both the facades as well as for the roof.

By favouring one idea instead of another this project enforces the ability of living in extremes.

Conceptual sketches

ABOVE AND BELOW: View of La Pérouse Hotel at 3 Allée du Quesne, Nantes; conceptual sketch

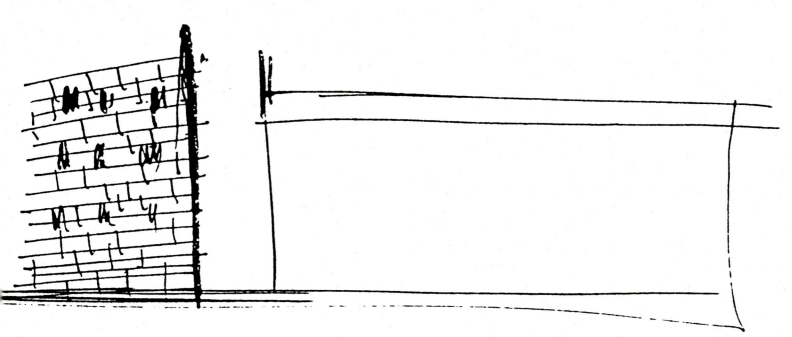

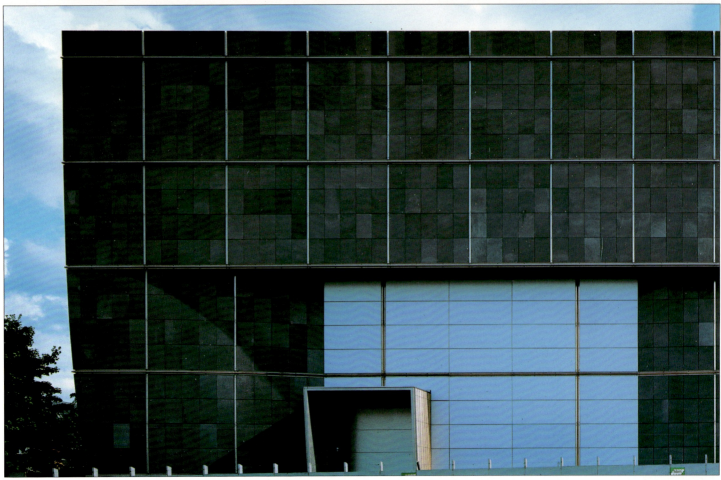

VAN BERKEL & BOS
50/10 KV DISTRIBUTING SUB-STATION
Amersfoort, The Netherlands

Essentially, the sub-station is little more than an almost entirely sealed container for three electrical transformers (50/10 kV). The polar division into two interlocking volumes is paralleled by the difference in claddings. The spatial encounters of the facade planes, through this polarity, which at times embraces a contextual dimension, refer to the invisible transformation process of electrical currents. The insulating basalt lava and the conductive aluminium present a contrast deepened by vertical and horizontal articulation.

Using light aluminium on the south face and darker basalt lava on the north explicates the spatial context. As the site is visible from many directions the relationship between spatial impact and cladding materials ultimately became one of the issues governing the design. The avoidance of specific detail by repeating link-ups between the materials shifts emphasis to the sculptural impact of the projecting and receding facade planes. The effect of depth created by the facades is perpetuated at a smaller scale in their subdivision by wooden rails set in steel. The only openings needed, namely the doors hoisting the transformers in and out, are also timber clad.

ABOVE AND BELOW: Conceptual sketch; perspective

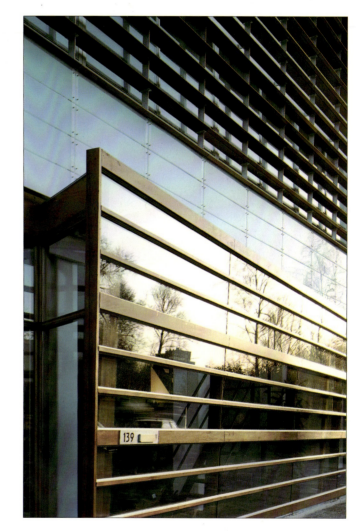

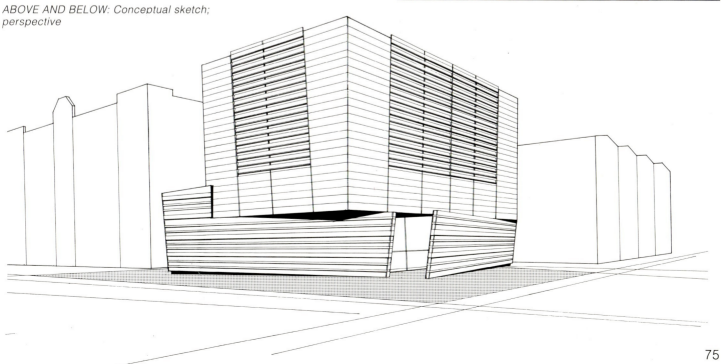

75

TONY FRETTON
PHOTOGRAPHER'S OFFICE
London

Anton, the photographer, makes videos and photographs of musicians, often on location, while his assistant remains to manage the office and his photographic archive, which is situated in a narrow mews in west London.

The ground floor, a generous working space and a dignified room in which to receive visitors, is filled with light from translucent windows facing the mews.

The components are arranged so that their shapes are part of a composition which extends through both of the floors. Their mass becomes apparent as you move around them, their forms rhyming with the strange forms of the telephone, photocopier and VDU monitors. When used, they are found to be purposeful in a straightforward way.

Traditional joinery techniques have been used for the cabinets, which hold the photographic archive, so that they are durable and practical. Yet the air this gives, of being deeply known, and the restless equality and numberlessness of the sliding drawers, make them surreal.

The stairway is a steep body-sized room into which light comes from a high space above. At the side, the kitchen is high and dark. Within the whole space different intensities and characters of space are experienced.

The upper floor is Anton's studio, with a small darkroom next to the stairway and a work table to hold his materials and equipment. A small light table is set into the end of the work surface so that he can refer to transparencies while working on a print. Space is left between this and the side wall so that he can sit facing a different direction, or someone else can work at the light table with him.

At times he will watch videos, show a client the work he has made or sit and reflect. The room can be lit either by two narrow spotlights in the ridge of the ceiling, concealed fluorescent lights which illuminate the ceiling with white light or colour it blue, or simply the light table.

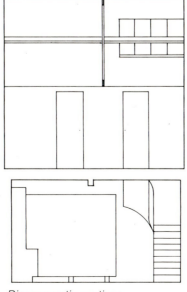

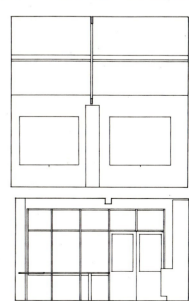

Diagrammatic sections

TOD WILLIAMS, BILLIE TSIEN AND ASSOCIATES
THE NEW COLLEGE, UNIVERSITY OF VIRGINIA
Charlottesville

New York City-based Tod Williams and Billie Tsien's commission to design dormitory space for 525 students and an adjacent dining hall, respected University founder Thomas Jefferson's ideas about creating enclosed outdoor spaces and his use of materials, but, on the given programme, their own perceptions and style were used.

The steep slope of the New College's 11-acre site did not permit a traditional four-sided quadrangle. Instead, the architects with Charlottesville-based David Oakland, of VMDO Architects, located the dining hall at the bottom of a 60-foot drop in grade and stepped the five dormitory blocks – in two pairs and a single – up the hill, a clear departure from Jefferson's 'academic village'. At the top of the hill is the principal's residence, which frames the outer edge of the College's own great lawn. A plaza in front of the dining hall connects to an adjacent 1985 dormitory, which shares the cafeteria. Pathways connect dormitories, including a winding pavement up the west side of the site that maintains less than a five per cent slope to accommodate wheelchair use without hand railings. Of the overall planning strategy the architects stated that the steeply sloping site was so far in time and space from the Jeffersonian lawn that it seemed more about the frontier, the edge, than the civilised containment of the terraced courtyard in the academic village.

Building heights vary from 30 to 40 feet because of the slope of the site; however, the overall effect is of low-slung retaining walls set into a cascading terrain. Pre-cast concrete floors and ceilings are framed by walls of concrete block with a ruddy brick facing. Flat roofs are edged with thick slate to emphasise the horizontality of the forms. Dormitories have double-loaded corridors with communal areas at each end. Rooms are primarily single-occupancy, but changes in grade provided space for some loft spaces and suites used as faculty apartments.

PIERRE D'AVOINE ARCHITECTS
THE WHITE HOUSE
London

Pierre d'Avoine's work at the White House in a London suburb proves his theory that every house, however ordinary it might seem, has something which makes it special. The White House has a lovely garden in which grow virginia creeper, ivy and a wisteria, clambering over the back of the building. The wisteria is at the heart of a project which has transformed the house and blurred the boundaries between the building and the garden, indoors and outdoors.

Formerly, the back part of the house was dark and cramped. Now it has been remodelled, extended and painted white so that the green garden is visible from the front door itself, at the end of a vista through a new series of open living spaces, full of north and west light. The only barrier between the house and garden is transparent, a glass screen of large sliding doors.

The kitchen is the fulcrum of the composition, treated as a service wall with one main free-standing work surface. The main living space is set down two steps, creating a slight separation between the two zones of activity. The dining space opens into a new enclosed courtyard on the west side, paved in concrete and tiny strops of stone and oak. A balcony and steel walkway above leads from the main bedroom suite around the edge of the courtyard and down a steel stairway straight into the garden. This stairway is shielded from the road by a high steel framework hung with heather screening, which will eventually be superseded by natural ivy growth.

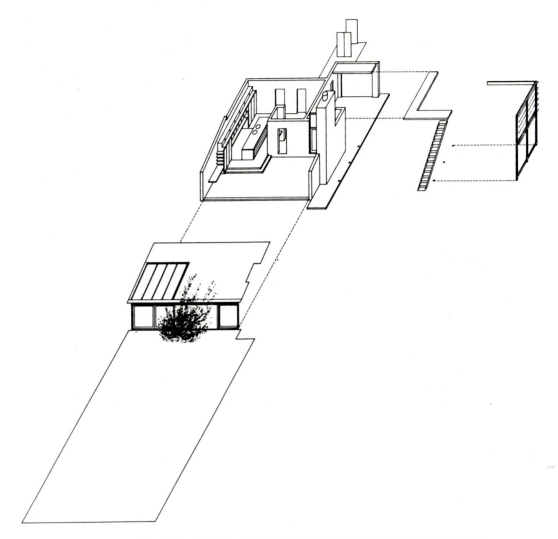

Exploded cut-away axonometric

DONALD JUDD
THE CHINATI FOUNDATION
Marfa, Texas

The group of buildings, that is now the property of the Chinati Foundation based just outside Marfa, has its origins in a former military base, Fort DA Russell. Included are two large old artillery sheds, ideally suited to the presentation of a group of Judd's major works of 1980-84, comprising one hundred rectangular aluminium boxes, arranged in three rows subdivided in various ways, and open on either one or two sides. There is also a large, broad-based aircraft hangar which later served as a gymnastics hall, still later as a riding hall (the 'Arena'), and which is today the site of festive gatherings of all kinds.

In addition, the complex includes numerous barracks which now provide space for administrative offices, the library, the printing shop, the school of painting for children, employees' living quarters and guest rooms for visitors and artists in residence. Most importantly, however, Judd's concept included present and future exhibition sites for the works of other artists.

In each case Judd restored and altered the long-abandoned and often severely damaged buildings through a process of purposeful intervention. As he stated, 'the gallery is fairly controllable, if limited, the public space slightly, the collector's glass ranch-house not at all'. Judd was critical of museums with their 'bad' architecture and 'thoughtless' policies, as well as the short duration of individual installations; for at the right place, once it had been found, a kind of partnership forms between the work of art and space.

Marfa provides the ideal museum where space, the quality and quantity of available light and the character of the surroundings play a significant role. With work at the same location, under different daylight conditions or with a change from daylight to artificial light, reunion exists which strengthens and deepens the impression.

USHIDA • FINDLAY PARTNERSHIP
TRUSS WALL HOUSE
Machida, Tokyo

The architects, Eisaku Ushida and Kathryn Findlay, seek to explore a fundamental relationship between the human body, its surroundings, space and perceptions. They integrate physical and sensory experiences aiming for what may be called 'cultural minimalism'. By working with the most primal forms and volumes (monochromatic and amorphous), and through continuous dialogue, the architects re-examine the interface between the consciousness and subconsciousness.

The Truss Wall House is named after a patented system of building compound-curve concrete. The commissioning brief allowed the architects to investigate the unexplored potential within the structural integrity, to create an open landscaped house which maximised the available site area – a slim and economic biomorphism. The architects were therefore asked to design a house on a small, awkwardly shaped site, in a difficult location in an exurb of Tokyo.

The house is curved and vertically sliced (by CAD) every 20cm. A truss was formed to the shape by bending reinforcing bars. These trusses are welded together laterally and covered with a fine wire mesh. Concrete is then poured into the hollow space between the trusses.

The design started by establishing a system which investigated the comfortability of the thermal environment – a thermodynamic organ. This was done with the use of a double-skin wall with insulation material, air cavities to exploit geothermal and solar heat and an earth layer on the roof garden which moderates the indoor temperature to a stable level.

Modernism has always rejected a malleable architectural material which can be formed to any shape; however, this building method presented the architects with a legitimate opportunity to industrially fabricate free-form concrete.

The house is a critique of Japanese urbanism, visually linked to the topography of the surrounding hills rather than the buildings in the street, *ergo* triggering a new consciousness in the city for both architects and local residents.

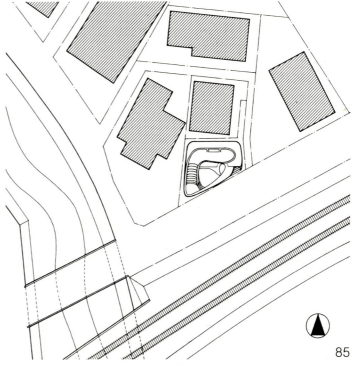

Site plan

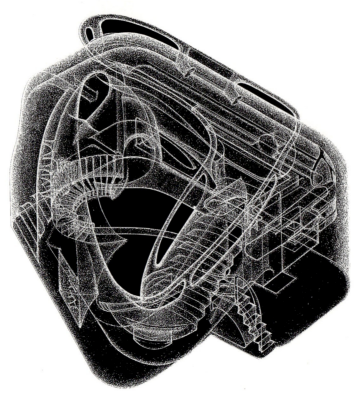

LEFT TO RIGHT: Worm's-eye axonometrics: transparently visceral drawings

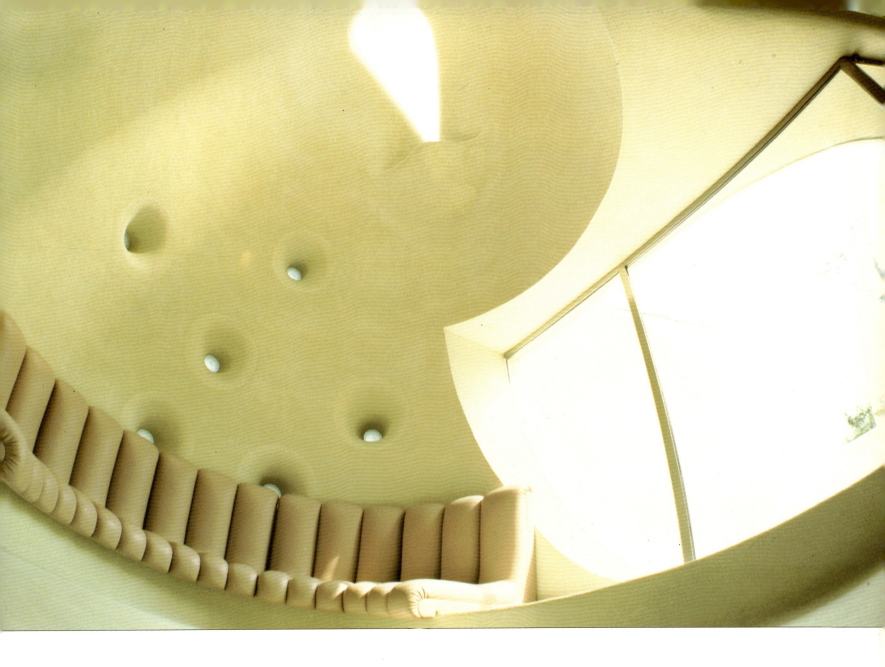
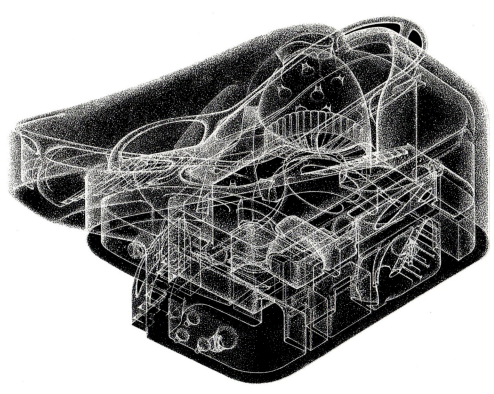

KATSUHIRO ISOBE
DISLOCATION: LANDSCAPING RING ZONES
Amsterdam

Sometimes a highway creates a forgotten space isolated by the transportation system itself. This site, in the south axis, Zuid-As, Amsterdam, is segregated on artificial land by the highway junctions, constructed canal, and river.

The main consideration is to transform this leftover space into a landscape which consists of shifted and undulating bands of houses; each with a narrow strip of garden on its roof. They work as noise protection and another dyke of the Amster River, while responding to the existing topographical context. The light of each dwelling filters through the side glass walls, revealing the landscape at night. Formerly isolated land on both sides of a highway is reconnected.

Dichotomies of movement exist between the site's man-made elements and the natural bend of the river. The design responds to these dynamic elements and develops a sensory experience. The landscape's undulation serves a dual purpose in its functionality and aesthetic play on these dichotomies. The shifted nature of the landscape further emphasises the dynamism of the site's contrasting qualities. Harmony is achieved.

Influential to the development of a design aesthetic has been the work of Aldo van Eyck, Herman Hertzberger and Giancarlo de Carlo – in terms of the strength of collectiveness; and the architecture of Frank Lloyd Wright. Most integral, however, is the Zen culture, as experienced in the Japanese rock garden. In the rock garden the natural order of the landscape elements and human imagination/thought are integral to each other. The sole elements are rock and sand: organisation is abstract and esoteric to Western logic, but specific to natural growth. Metaphors for life arise and posit layers of interpretation; for instance, rocks and sand may symbolise landscape and the sea.

These metaphors apply specifically to the architecture of Isobe. The underlying principle he states is 'You can get much from so little . . . beauty lies in simplicity'.

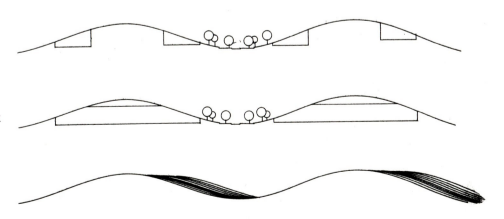

OPPOSITE: *The landscape of man: house forms respond to topography of site;* ABOVE: *Undulating form of new terrain;* CENTRE: *Unit with roof garden;* BELOW: *Dwelling unit; pathway; external linearity*

O'HERLIHY + WARNER
O'HERLIHY HOUSE
Malibu, California

The design of the O'Herlihy House aspires towards the rigour and restraint of modernism, while it also celebrates the tactile quality of crafted materials. The house, which sits on a canyon-side plateau with spectacular ocean and mountain views, is tied integrally to the landscape and is, at the same time, in direct contrast to it.

Its relationship to the landscape is expressed metaphorically by the organisation of the two major axes: one axis is orientated towards the canyon, the other towards the ocean. However, the white, unadorned volumes deliberately contrast with the landscape, asserting their architectural independence.

The interior and exterior spaces of the house interpenetrate, creating a continual dialogue with the natural surroundings. The thick plaster walls, Mexican tile floors and beamed ceilings are warm and rustic in character, yet reductive and refined in their execution.

RIGHT: South elevation; site plan; BELOW: Isometric

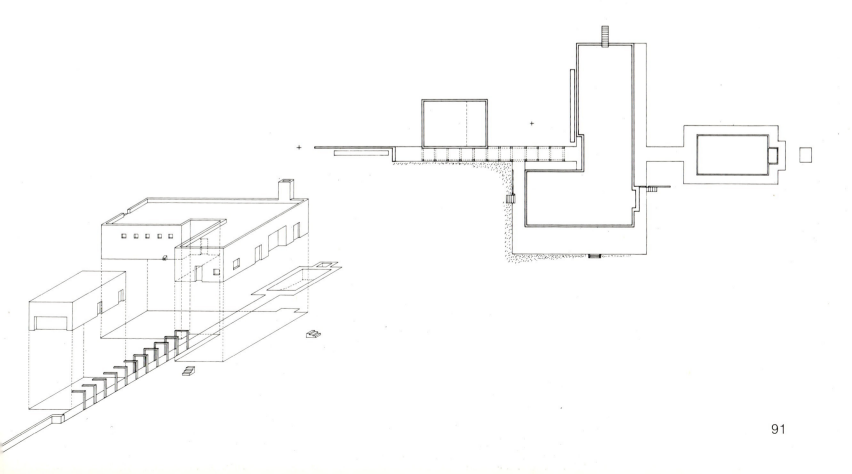

TADAO ANDO
VITRA SEMINAR HOUSE
Germany

This seminar house was designed for a furniture company which produces a broad line of furniture by designers of both traditional and contemporary renown, such as Charles Eames, Mario Bellini and Philippe Starck. The building, located near the company's production facility in southern Germany, accommodates various company activities, from employee training to conferences.

The principal focus of the project was the positioning of the building and its path of approach on the site, which is extremely flat. The architect chose to minimise the building on the site and to situate part of its volume underground. Using simple geometric forms – circles and squares – he formed a composition of contrasting volumes and voids, and sought to generate a rich interior space.

Located nearby, on the same site, is the Vitra Design Museum by Frank Gehry. Selecting an orientation for the building that would achieve harmony and balance with the Design Museum without disturbing the existing trees on the site – and with a sculpture by Claes Oldenburg located between the buildings – required careful deliberation.

Visitors make a circuitous loop around the Museum, past the outdoor sculpture and approach the building along an L-shaped wall. Three elements comprise the building: a rectangular volume running parallel to the walls of the square sunken court; a rectangular volume which penetrates the court at an angle of 60 degrees and a cylindrical volume, forming a spatial void, that interlocks with the two rectilinear volumes.

The building has two levels accommodating conference rooms, a library, private rooms and a lobby – all open into the tranquillity of the sunken court. Inset into the flat site, the sunken court functions as a device for luring and retaining the elements of nature – light and wind – within all spaces of the building. Nature imbues the architecture with colour, lending orchestration to daily life.

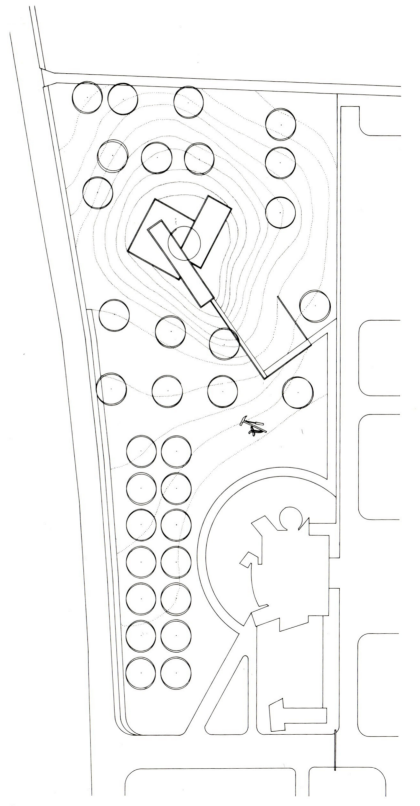

Site plan

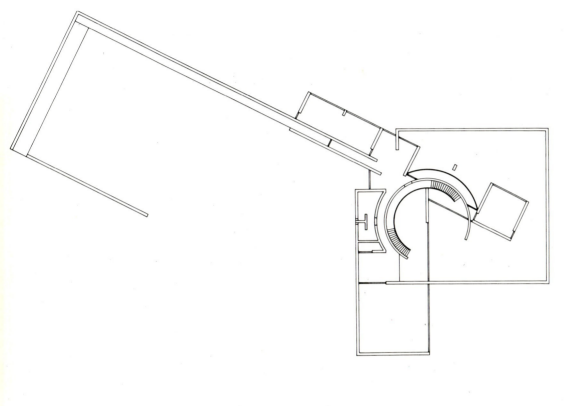

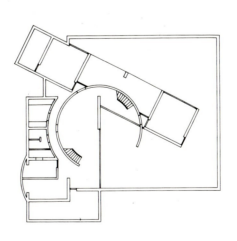

95